YO! PICASSO!

Beside Picasso

T0315845

Brian McAvera

YO! PICASSO!

Beside Picasso

OBERON BOOKS
LONDON

First published in 2002 by Oberon Books Ltd.
(incorporating Absolute Classics)
521 Caledonian Road, London N7 9RH
Tel: 020 7607 3637 / Fax: 020 7607 3629
e-mail: oberon.books@btinternet.com
www.oberonbooks.com

Copyright © Brian McAvera 2002

Brian McAvera is hereby identified as author of this work in
accordance with section 77 of the Copyright, Designs and
Patents Act 1988. The author has asserted his moral rights.

All rights whatsoever in this play including film, television, radio
and electronic rights are strictly reserved and application for
performance etc. should be made before rehearsal to The
Sharland Organisation, The Manor House, Manor Street,
Raunds, Northamptonshire NN9 6JW, Tel: 01933 626600, Fax:
01933 624860 Email: tsoshar@aol.com. No performance may be
given unless a licence has been obtained, and no alterations may
be made in the title or the text of the play without the author's
prior written consent.

This book is sold subject to the condition that it shall not by
way of trade or otherwise be circulated without the publisher's
consent in any form of binding or cover other than that in which
it is published and without a similar condition including this
condition being imposed on any subsequent purchaser.

A catalogue record for this book is available from the British
Library.

ISBN: 1 84002 347 3

Cover design: Malcolm Cochrane

Contents

The author wishes to thank warmly Mick Jasper and Iain Armstrong of AJTC, not only for commissioning the play, but also for giving him the luxury of workshopping it at various stages in its genesis; also Geoff Bullen, the director, who has been associated with the project from first draft stage; 'Maltings Art Centre, Farnham'; Doug Holton of London Live, and Angus McKechnie of the National Theatre, London, both of whom showcased the production; the Royal Society of Authors who provided a gratefully received grant; and to Una, Rachel and Sarah who put up with me 'being somewhere else'.

And to Tot Taylor, the composer, for providing superb music for the second tour.

Author's Note

This is a play for two male actors. Picasso plays himself, but also plays many of the women that he lived with. Sabartés plays himself, but also a host of other characters who come into contact with Picasso. The actors are intended to snap into their characters, deriving fricative energy from the immediate switchback between one character and another.

However, this is *not* simply a play in which actors play multiple roles. Rather it is a play in which the only way of getting *at* the material of the play resides in a highly functional use of multiple role-playing.

Picasso was, to say the least, an inveterate womaniser. One of the subjects of the play is his relationship with women and the use that he made of women, both in his personal life, and in his art. In quarrying these aspects of sexuality, power and violence, it seemed to me to be quite wrong to have an actress play the female roles. The physical presence of a female body, especially a female body required to participate in various scenes of a sexual nature, would conjure up all kinds of reactions which I did not want *interfering* with the thrust of a given scene. In a Brechtian sense, the advantage of having a man play the female role is that he can *demonstrate* the function of the character in that scene, without having the stimulus/response reaction that men will bring to a female body.

All of the role-playing is thematically functional, and often emblematic. Sabartés' ultimate job is to bring Picasso to a realisation that his *use* of the women is morally wrong. To that end he is prepared to try various strategies. When either of them 'enters' a character, that character can have various degrees of *transparency*. By this I mean that the play is in the form of a serious game. Sabartés tries various strategies, usually requiring Picasso to assume a role (often that of one of the women). The aim of each of these game-plays is to get Picasso to see things from the point of view of that individual.

But Picasso rapidly becomes aware of the game, and although he doesn't initially know where the game is leading, being a natural games-player, he participates enthusiastically and is determined to win. When he inhabits a character, he can do so with various degrees of fullness or transparency. At one end of the scale he may merely demonstrate with extreme sketchiness, so that we, the audience, remain only too aware of the character of *Picasso* using or manipulating the *role-character* for his own ends. At the other end of the scale he can be forced to *become* the role-character so that his own character does not obtrude at all. This sounds complicated in theory but is actually perfectly feasible for an actor to achieve.

The game has multiple levels in that both Picasso and Sabartés regularly play off the audience, trying to build up sympathy for themselves, each at the expense of the other. Both characters, once locked into the game, also take advantage of the rules to the fullest extent so that, for example, at crucial points, Sabartés will role-play Picasso, or vice-versa, as each jockeys for advantage.

At another level, as becomes clear towards the end of the play, the role-playing becomes additionally emblematic in that it is suggested that the relationship between Sabartés and Picasso – at least from the point of view of Sabartés – contained a strongly repressed homo-erotic aspect.

This particular style of *playing* demands absolute clarity on behalf of the actors and director. The material is complex and requires an audience to *work,* as not only do the actors inhabit numerous characters to various and shifting degrees, but they also inhabit a time-scale which can range at will over a period of almost ninety years, as well as inhabiting numerous locales.

Clearly we are in the realm of non-naturalistic theatre. In my view, no theatre is absolutely realistic/naturalistic, or absolutely non-naturalistic. It operates along a sliding scale, according to the demands of the playwright, the audience, and the historical period. There is absolutely no reason why naturalistic sequences (or even lines) cannot co-exist easily with non-naturalistic sequences. The key element is that the conventions developed by the playwright should be consistent in terms of the world of the play; and thus the acting and directorial conventions need to be equally consistent.

All acting and writing is, to a degree, role-playing. This particular play simply ups the ante, so to speak. It uses various theatrical forms which *seem* to function as if they were asides, soliloquies, reported speech or exposition, flashbacks, and so own. I would contend that these are inadequate labels. *Exposition*, for example, is one of those words used to belabour playwrights. Generally it simply means 'giving the audience the necessary information so that they may understand the plot, characters etc.'. Often it is used pejoratively as if the giving of 'information' were somehow inadequate. One should give the 'information' dramatically, *through* the structure. The problem is that critics rarely recognise the difference between exposition, and something which looks, on the surface, as if it is exposition.

For example, in *Yo! Picasso: Beside Picasso*, Picasso seemingly describes a portrait that he painted of Sabartés. On the surface this looks like exposition: straightforward description or information.

Yet it very definitely isn't. For a start it tells us, in terms of the *language,* how Picasso saw and felt about Sabartés at that moment in time. Its texture and rhythms lightly sketch in a sensuous appreciation of Sabartés' body, as if he were a woman, thus prefiguring the suppressed homo-erotic element that emerges towards the end of the play. The weight of this section, as well as its placement and juxtaposition, indicate that this is an oil-painting of Sabartés (and thus an indication of how important Sabartés has become for Picasso) as opposed to the quick pencil or charcoal sketch such as that exhibited less than a year earlier in Barcelona.

In terms of staging, this play is constructed to be played as fluently as possible. It is perfectly feasible to play it minimally with just four or five chairs used to indicate varying locations. Other suggestions are indicated in the text.

Music is important. Apart from the few specific references in the text (Spanish bullfight music; the Debussy) I would suggest that a contemporary composer should be used to provide the punctuation points. Likewise the humour is important: the lighter it is played, especially in the opening act, the better.

Obviously the degree of literalism in the setting will influence the degree of literalism in the acting. For example, as written, most of the actions, such as painting, drawing, laying a table or whatever, are meant to be mimed by the actors, and this minimalism in the acting suits a miminalist staging. The more the staging shifts into the direction of verisimilitude, the more veristic – in the Stanislavskian sense – the acting needs to be.

Although this play is called *Yo! Picasso: Beside Picasso*, and although Picasso, Sabartés, and all of the others were real people, and although the basic details, in so far as they are knowable, are essentially correct, this is my construction of these people. I was not remotely interested in biography. The broad themes of the work – sex, art, power – are timeless and universal, the stuff of airport paperbacks as well as real literature. I wanted this play to connect to contemporary audiences, just as Picasso's work does. As such the language quite deliberately shifts in and out of numerous different registers, sliding easily from demotic, idiomatic, naturalistic or slangy vernaculars to various versions of what I hope is a supple, dense and poetically charged prose.

I see no reason to underestimate an audience: if one entertains them, they are perfectly prepared to allow you the latitude of dangerous, difficult and dense subject-matter. I have tried to make the mechanism of the form into a kind of roller-coaster. At the end of the first half, the audience is exhausted and exhilarated – but they are now in possession of the raw material of the play. Then can then sit back, like a passenger on a rollercoaster, and hurtle towards the destination.

Characters

PICASSO

SABARTÉS

Yo! Picasso! was first performed at The Farnham Maltings Art Centre, Surrey, on 16 September 1999, with the following cast:

PABLO PICASSO, Iain Armstrong

JAIME SABARTÉS, Mick Jasper

Designer, Maz Bullen

Director, Geoff Bullen

The play was commissioned and first produced by AJTC and toured the UK in 1999–2000, including The Pleasance Theatre, London. It also appeared as part of the National Theatre, London season of *Picasso's Women* in the Platform series at the Cottlesloe, produced by Barbara Flynn & Angus McKechnie, and in a showcase performance at the Bridewell Theatre, London, under the aegis of London Live, courtesy Doug Holton, followed by the Edinburgh Festival that year, then Belfast Festival, then at the Stadssehoupburg, Amsterdam. It toured again in 2002–3 and is scheduled to tour in the Netherlands in 2004.

Darkness: a thick palpable darkness.

Over the following images of the major women in PICASSO's life, the eerie sound of wind as if on a deserted street, with eddies catching paper litter and scraping it along the ground.

A light slices through the darkness, suddenly and all-too-briefly illuminating, centre stage and halfway to the Gods, a suspended head of Fernande, PICASSO's first long-term mistress. The head, more a rounded mask perhaps than head, is a paeon of well-rounded sensuousness. To her left a brief illumination of Eva, a slender ethereal vision of Japanese-style prettiness. To her right Gaby, a wholesome outdoor beauty. To Eva's left Olga with her sharp-featured prettiness; to Gaby's right the voluptuous blonde Marie-Thérèse, to Olga's left the 'weeping woman' of Dora; to Marie-Thérèse's right the schoolgirl ponytail of Françoise, to Françoise's right the scarfed head of Jacqueline.

The illumination vanishes. The wind ceases. Darkness. A beat. There is a jaunty drumroll, the equally jaunty music of the circus and a spot downstage centre flares into life. Coming towards it as if towards a mirage in the desert, all of his senses on the alert PICASSO, dressed in a sailor's jersey, finds his arm snaking into the spot, and a piece of white paper emerging from his hand as if by magic. Then he finds himself standing frontally in the spot. A beat: is this really the place that he used to know so well? He grins.

PICASSO: Used to come here a lot. The Cirque Medrano. Lion-tamers, elephants…riding-girls…trapeze artists in long legs, spangles and narrow breasts, acrobats and clowns…my *saltimbanques.*

Reminded me of home…the troupes of tumblers, fire-eaters and the upright bear…

Good place to get into the skirts of a woman.

He folds the paper, tearing into it, like a conjuror.

Women love dexterity, artifice, style…a bit of mystery –

With a flourish he produces a row of cut-out female figures: he is surprised at his lack of artistic ability.

Another hand reaches into the spot, snatches the cut-outs, and crumples them. The body follows: it is SABARTÉS. The following has the speed, pace, energy, timing and humour of a music-hall routine. It has all the energy of a game, the rules of which only one player, SABARTÉS, initially knows.

(*A doubletake.*) You can't do that!

You?… You're Sabartés! You're my pet poodle!

SABARTÉS: Your confidant –

PICASSO: My dogsbody, my lickspittle –

SABARTÉS: Your witness –

PICASSO: My scapegoat, my little arse-licking, blind-as-a-bat –

SABARTÉS: Secretary –

PICASSO: – piss-on-my-command wanker!

You treasure every scrap I ever dropped.

You'd frame a turd if I gave it to you!

SABARTÉS: Not up here I don't.

Smartly boxes PICASSO's cheeks. PICASSO is rooted to the spot: stunned

(*To the audience; ruminatively.*) I've all to play for…yet so little time…

PICASSO: You can't slap me!

SABARTÉS: I can't?

PICASSO: No!

SABARTÉS: Oh!…

Slaps PICASSO's face again – hard! A sideways glance to the audience. Then decisively slides a chair towards PICASSO.

Sit!

PICASSO does so, like an automaton.

Good boy! (*To the audience.*) Ladies and gentlemen, this is Pablo Ruiz Picasso, God help him.

(*Gleefully.*) And he won't!

Good boy!

Lovingly boxes him on the cheeks again.

PICASSO: But you...the first time we met you...

You *wrote*... 'My eyes were dazzled. I was ready to bow, stunned by the magic power that emanated from his whole being...'

SABARTÉS: (*To audience.*) Bullshit!

(*To PICASSO.*) Still in shock? Tough!

(*To audience.*) Tonight, we take you on a trip.

(*Points to PICASSO.*) In here, a penis. A widely-travelled penis.

Imagine each penetrative erection as a six-inch slash of white.

Lay them end to end and they'd stretch from here to the Acropolis – and back!

PICASSO: (*Pointing to audience.*) Who are they?

SABARTÉS: Get used to them. We only exist when they're here.

PICASSO: (*Flexing his wrist.*) You forget.

(*Imperiously.*) I create. I exist through that.

SABARTÉS: Not up here you don't. You created. Past tense. I was the biographer...hagiographer... Past tense.

PICASSO: And present tense?

SABARTÉS: In the present tense?

You're fucked!

Beat.

Are you sorry for what you've done?

PICASSO: (*Reflexively.*) Piss off!

But SABARTÉS is already walking away. PICASSO takes a few steps in his direction, reaches out towards him.

(*Appalled at his condition.*) I can't work…

SABARTÉS: (*Beat.*) Well let's see if we can't change that…

Snaps his fingers: music – possibly Albeniz – the stage is backlit, revealing a vast jumble of objects heaped up in seeming disorder: paintings, books, Disques Bleus cartons.

Barcelona. 1899.

Keynote for this sequence: seeming nostalgic longing for youthful good times. PABLO snaps into assertive mode. SABARTÉS dons thick-rimmed glasses, acquires a slight hunch, becomes myopic, takes off his coat to reveal a typical turn-of-the-century dandy. Fussing like a mother hen as he holds up a velvet jacket for PABLO to put on.

You'll need your coat Pablo. It's cold outside. You'll get a chill.

Hands him a walking cane.

PICASSO: (*Putting on coat: to audience.*) Nag nag nag.

You'd think he was my mother; or my wife.

SABARTÉS: (*To audience.*) At least he takes care of his clothes. Properly pressed trousers. Starched shirt. Stylish cravat. (*Dryly.*) Rather flamboyant choice of hats. He lacks a proper sense of decorum.

PICASSO is twirling the walking cane impatiently.

Unlike myself, Catalan you see, he doesn't come from well-bred stock – Andalusian – but I don't hold it against him.

(*Almost as an afterthought.*) To us, an Andalusian suggests a bullfighter, a wide boy, a gypsy who drinks and dances the flamenco.

(*Looking at PICASSO.*) Someone with a short jacket, tight trousers, big cock, Cordoban felt hat and ever so many cock-and-bull stories.

Ugh!

PICASSO: Stop primping your moustache Jaimes. Els Quatre Gats and then the brothel.

Or the brothel and then Els Quatre Gats?

SABARTÉS: Coffee?

PICASSO: (*Speeding away.*) The brothel it is!

Music: the Tango.

(*Pool of red light.*) Ah! Conchita Escuelda Morales. The love of my life!

Arse in the air please. Oh, yes!

Right Jaimes.

SABARTÉS: Eh?

PICASSO: Mount her for fuck's sake! (*Alternative: 'for Christ's sake'*)

Bewildered, SABARTÉS obeys, unzips his flies and 'mounts' her. As he does so PICASSO whips out a sketchbook from his pocket and starts to draw them in the act.

Okay. Rosie, you can start on me now!

Unzips his flies for oral sex.

(*To SABARTÉS.*) Don't come too quick Jaimes, I need at least forty seconds!

He is sketching rapidly.

SABARTÉS: (*Moving rapidly into a rhythm towards climax.*) That's – not – possible – with – Conchita...

PICASSO: (*Moving towards climax.*) Yes – it – is.

A fuck for art's sake.

Art for fuck's sake.

Oh...Jesus! My pencil's an ejaculation of the wrist!

SABARTÉS: Jesus –

PICASSO: (*Screaming.*) Hold it! Almost there!

SABARTÉS: (*Screaming.*) I can't! I'm getting there!

PICASSO/SABARTÉS: (*Ululating.*) We're there!

They both collapse onto their knees. SABARTÉS, on his knees, makes his way over to PICASSO, zipping up his flies as he goes. The tango fades.

SABARTÉS: (*Looking down at the drawing. Accusingly.*) My arse is more compact than that.

PICASSO: The cheeks of your arse compact with the effort; then distend. I draw what I see.

SABARTÉS: (*Flicking back a page of the sketchbook.*) Why didn't you draw them as they compacted?

PICASSO: When your bum distends, your belly sags.

A neat visual rhyme. Better composition.

SABARTÉS: What about my dignity?

PICASSO: What's dignity got to do with art?

You want me to draw like an old man? Society portraits?

SABARTÉS: (*Beat. Hanging his head.*) And he rarely did.

(*To audience. He is almost jealous.*) Always the sketchbook.

Couples kiss, men piss in the gutter; a funeral carriage trundles past a man with a scythe, stray faces looking in upon the margins… Young girls undressing as a Peeping Tom longs for a touch. Three drawings offered for ten pesetas.

Total sale: Nada!!!

PICASSO: (*Glancing at SABARTÉS; then to audience.*) You couldn't call him handsome, but it's imperfection that makes for interesting art.

Look!

Squares a frame in the air, as if about to start painting a portrait. SABARTÉS is sitting, as if for his portrait.

Chestnut-coloured hair, long and smooth, falling over his shoulders into half-hearted curls.

A loose-fitting corduroy jacket with a round collar, buttoned up at the neck. Pince-nez.

Thick lips, spatulate nose, a moustache that two tons of manure couldn't stimulate into growth…and the dreamy air of a plaintive little-boy-lost.

SABARTÉS: (*Leaping to his feet.*) Which is how the bastard painted me: Barcelona 1900!

PICASSO: Bastard? Bastard? You're very free with your language after a lifetime of verbal probity!

SABARTÉS: Verbal probity? *Moral* probity!

Kahnweiler. Paris. 1947.

PICASSO: (*Beginning to see the possibilities of the game.*)
I liked Kahnweiler.

SABARTÉS: You liked baiting Kahnweiler.

PICASSO: Rubbish!

SABARTÉS: You betrayed Kahnweiler.

PICASSO: Preposterous.

SABARTÉS: (*To audience.*) Oh yes?

> *Music cue: Overly Germanic – Wagnerian, or else with a slight parodic edge.*

> *To PICASSO, as Kahnweiler. Ramrod-straight. Cultured voice. Very calm, no matter what. Slight German accent. His accentuation, inflexions and stress patterns are those of a non-native speaker of 'French'. Playing the game.*

> Herr Picasso. How delightful to see you once again.

PICASSO: (*Beat.*) Oh I see! You're *pretending* to be Kahnweiler.

> Very good! Why, you've got him to a T!

> Monsieur Kahnweiler. How gracious of you to visit.

> (*Beat.*) Nothing for you, I'm afraid.

SABARTÉS: (*As Kahnweiler.*) I see you have Monsieur Carré in attendance.

PICASSO: I was thinking of offering him some of the major works.

> He's become so…dependable.

SABARTÉS: (*As Kahnweiler.*) Major works? I thought those were reserved for me.

PICASSO: Kootz arrives from New York tomorrow.

Will buy as much as I'm prepared to sell him – and at my unit price…

SABARTÉS: (*As Kahnweiler.*) How nice for Monsieur Kootz.

(*Carefully playing the game.*) If Monsieur Kootz or Monsieur Carré can afford to buy your work at inflated prices, good luck to them.

I have to make a profit. I have to create a clientele. I have an artist to service.

An artist who likes money, and at regular intervals.

PICASSO: When I think about it, in my early days, didn't you exploit me in the most shameless manner possible!

SABARTÉS: (*As Kahnweiler.*) No.

I seem to remember you remarking. In order for paintings to be sold at very high prices, they must first have been sold at very low prices. Correct?

PICASSO: You are an exploiter! You've never given a damm about me!

SABARTÉS: (*As Kahnweiler.*) Really?

(*Almost enjoying himself.*) I seem to remember, a long time ago now, Wilhelm Uhde telling me about a strange Assryrian picture that…*someone*…was painting.

(*To audience.*) Max Jacob eventually nicknamed it *Les Démoiselles d'Avignon.*

So one day in 1907 I set off for Montmartre, climb the hill, find this *Bateau Lavoir* studio hanging off the top like a carbuncle on a nose, and walk down, down to this Picasso's studio.

Lighting change: we are now in 1907.

PICASSO: (*Determined to win: enthusiastically enters this new phase of the game.*)

(*As Younger Self: shirt open to waist. Surveys him.*) Dealer?

Kahnweiler nods. PICASSO takes his arm and leads him in.

Kahnweiler is looking around with distaste.

(*Taking the piss with a straight face.*) Wallpaper tatters: latest vogue in decoration.

The mountain of ashes beside the stove? That's for mixing with clay; gives a grittier texture to the sculpture.

No, this is not a couch with a hole in it. *This* is interior decoration with a cooling updraft.

This? It's what I'm working on at the moment.

Nobody likes it.

Even my 'friend' Braque said it made him feel as if someone were drinking petrol and spitting out fire.

SABARTÉS: (*As Kahnweiler.*) I don't think you're interested in painting pretty pictures. So liking is irrelevant.

PICASSO: (*Aware that this is a different kind of intelligence.*) But you wouldn't want to buy it, would you?

SABARTÉS: (*Decisively. As Kahnweiler.*) I would.

PICASSO: (*Beat.*) Well it's not for sale.

SABARTÉS: (*As Kahnweiler.*) Of course not. It's not finished. If an artist is going to explore a new dimension, he must live with the consequences until the new geography emerges.

But I will buy other work.

(*Beat.*) Now.

1907 lighting change disappears.

PICASSO: (*Dryly.*) Very good. You can get up now.

SABARTÉS: Before Kahnweiler, it was a different story. Wasn't it?

PICASSO: (*Mockingly.*) Oh! When I was young you mean. Young and indigent.

SABARTÉS: And carefree. Els Quatre Gats.

Your first exhibition –

PICASSO: Hah! A hundred and fifty portraits on scraps of paper, pinned up on the walls of the cafe like soldiers on parade!

My My My!

SABARTÉS: (*Smugly. Seeing them.*) Me!

PICASSO: You.

Just about everyone I knew. In fact, half of Barcelona! Sketched from the life.

SABARTÉS: Where they would be seen by Ramon Casas, Santiago Rusiñol, Utrillo, Canals, Nonell, Pere Romeu –

PICASSO: And every other artist back from Paris.

One to five pesetas each!

SABARTÉS: (*Innocently.*) May as well have given them away…

PICASSO: I only ever keep the best.

Barcelona is too small, too provincial.

It was time to leave. For Paris.

SABARTÉS: (*To PICASSO.*) But you left without me.

PICASSO: Didn't I immortalise you?

Didn't I paint your portrait again and again?

SABARTÉS: Not *that* often.

PICASSO: Do you remember the first portrait I did of you before you went off to South America?

SABARTÉS: (*Unwillingly being drawn in.*) You were grumpy, bored and –

PICASSO: – I said, 'I'm going to paint you.

Do you want me to?

Of course, you later interpreted the painting masterfully in your books: how I was on the eve of a revolutionary development; the implication that the coloration of your rosy lips heralded the Rose period…

SABARTÉS: Which was bullshit.

Introduce bullfight music, and throughout the following gradually introduce crowd cheering. This sequence should have PICASSO as the bull, in every sense, with SABARTÉS as the toreador. The action is choreographed with all the fervour, élan and bloodlust of the corrida itself.

PICASSO: Surely not!

SABARTÉS: Shall I tell you how later critics described it, Pablo?

(*Bitter irony slowly seeping through.*) Supercilious eyebrows. Huge fleshy lips and myopic eyes; a provincial dandy; a sardonic, twistedly affectionate portrayal of pretentiousness, mercilessly observed and assessed…mocked…

PICASSO: (*Deadpan.*) Which was bullshit.

SABARTÉS: Surely not! I was the scapegoat, wasn't I, for all the others? And I didn't see it.

Too blind. Too myopic. Too stupid. Too wrapped up in my own pretensions.

For a brief moment PICASSO stretches out his hand as if to touch SABARTÉS on the sleeve. Then he abruptly withdraws it.

PICASSO: (*Gruffly, leg pawing the ground like a bull.*) I paint what I see.

SABARTÉS: (*Riposting. Whipping out bullfighter's red 'flag'.*) You paint as you feel.

PICASSO: (*With intense seriousness, one 'hoof' stamping the ground in slow fierceness.*) Others interpret.

You had – still have – a life through me.

SABARTÉS: (*Circling.*) You acquired – still do – the status of legend, through me.

(*Stabs and misses.*) I created you!

PICASSO: Really?

SABARTÉS: I dramatised you. I wrote the myths.

PICASSO: – Which I provided for you.

SABARTÉS: (*Stabs and misses.*) And I embellished and gave currency to!

PICASSO: And didn't we both benefit? Didn't we both gain power?

SABARTÉS: Equally?

PICASSO: I had the talent. The genius.

SABARTÉS: I had talents.

PICASSO: Of course you had –

27

SABARTÉS: Which is why you described me as a failure.

PICASSO: (*Airily.*) I always exaggerate. You know that.

SABARTÉS: (*Circling.*) I was a poet. Not a very good one. But I learnt.

I was a painter and a sculptor, but my eyes were weak. However, it taught me how to see; how to recognize the real thing.

I was a journalist for thirty years, writing for the major European newspapers, producing two books on politics and foreign affairs.

I was a novelist, published in South America, Spain and France.

All of which I gave up – to help you.

PICASSO: (*Lunging: the first 'goring' by the bull.*) Not to mention giving up a wife and a handicapped child. Left behind in Barcelona…

Convenient.

SABARTÉS: *I* was your critic and biographer, writing essays, prefaces, articles, books – but to you I had no talent, other than that of being useful *to* you.

PICASSO: (*Circling.*) But that was one of your greatest talents, Jaime! Didn't it take most of the world a half a century or more to recognize me for what I am: a genius who revolutionised the way the world *looks* at the world? You recognized it from the start.

True?

SABARTÉS: (*Unwillingly.*) True…in its way…I recognized a talent that was different from the provincial.

PICASSO: You recognized the fully-fledged emergence of a genius.

SABARTÉS: (*A second score.*) No.

PICASSO: What do you mean 'No'?

SABARTÉS: That's what I wrote. That's what you told me. There's a difference.

PICASSO: (*Contemptuously.*) What difference?

SABARTÉS: The difference between the reality and the myth. Your peers didn't recognize you as exceptional.

PICASSO: (*Exasperated.*) What differences?

SABARTÉS: That you walked upright from the moment you were a toddler?

PICASSO: I did!

SABARTÉS: Myth! And that sweet tale of your father – how, when you were fourteen, your artist father renounced his profession because of your genius, handing over to you his paints, his palette, and his brushes, never to paint again!

PICASSO: He did!

SABARTÉS: No he didn't. He kept on painting until his eyesight failed!

What else have we? Oh yes. That such was your youthful expertise, that you passed the three-day entrance examination to The Royal Academy of San Fernando with astonishing rapidity – in a single day in fact – in such a way that your examiners were utterly astonished. You could draw like Raphael!

PICASSO: I did!

SABARTÉS: No astonishing rapidity. No astonished examiners. No budding Raphael. Just a pass.

You had to work for it son. A spittle of inspiration and a torrent of perspiration.

PICASSO: (*Beat: slowly.*) Bullshit!

SABARTÉS: Yes. You're full of it.

After this final stab with twin knives, the bull collapses to its knees. SABARTÉS, the victor, triumphantly slices off the bull's ear and displays it to the crowd, triumphantly soliciting their approval. But the following will lead to an unexpected goring by the bull.

PICASSO: 1935!

What were you?

Back from South America.

Couldn't hack it, could you?

It was me offered you a job, and immortality.

(*To audience.*) I'll say that again.

(*To SABARTÉS.*) Immortality!

End of bullfight music.

And I didn't just do your picture in paint, did I?

I did it in poetry. I wrote you what you meant to me.

Produces sheet from his person like a conjuror – illuminated by a blaze of light. Quotes from the sheet though it is clear he knows the poem off by heart: with each quotation SABARTÉS is gored.

Luminescent coal of friendship.

Quickened by the breath of a kiss on the hand.

As true in the telling as the certainty of a clock –

As sweet –

SABARTÉS: – 'as the caress of a breath on a hand'. (*Holding up his hand.*) Bad poetry!

PICASSO: True words.

SABARTÉS: Weasel words.

PICASSO: True words *and* weasel words. Because that's the way I am.

(*Spitting it out.*) Son!

SABARTÉS: (*Deliberately.*) Fuck you.

PICASSO: I always did. You always bent over.

That was your contribution. Your character!

SABARTÉS: And what –

PICASSO: Love.

I loved you – just like any of the women.

SABARTÉS is staring coldly at him.

Okay. I inseminated you.

SABARTÉS: You rolled the women over, opened their legs and took them.

Or you opened their legs and ate them.

Or you had them open your legs and suck you – or should it be 'sucked up to you?'

PICASSO: You should know.

SABARTÉS: I do know. Now.

PICASSO: You always knew. You wanted a hero. You needed to worship.

And I...needed you.

A great artist needs a great biographer.

You!

For a moment SABARTÉS begins to preen.

And a permanent arselicker.

Remember that article you wrote – when you followed me – eventually, to Paris?

SABARTÉS: Oh…yes…

PICASSO: You were so shocked by the new work; its 'shrieking' colours, its flatness and simplifications.

SABARTÉS: (*Quickly.*) But I learnt to understand it.

PICASSO: Which is why, when that English journalist from *The Studio* came along to interview me, I asked instead that you read him your essay.

SABARTÉS: (*Equally dryly.*) It was written in Castillian!

But I did.

PICASSO: Beautifully! What was it you said?

Lighting change: we are back in turn-of-the-century Paris. SABARTÉS is in lecturer-mode, reading his article. PICASSO, as the journalist is in a chair, solemnly listening to him.

SABARTÉS: 'Picasso's art emanates from sadness and grief and pain. Life, that valley of tears, is at the core of the artist's work which is a form of instinctive self-expression – '

PICASSO: (*As English journalist.*) Top-hole old boy!

SABARTÉS: ' – a riverbed for that shower of blue tears.

An artist must be innocent, instinctive – (*Journalist begins to nod off.*) – exploring the relationship between colour and feeling, developing an, anti-theoretical theory (*Journalist is now snoring.*) which demonstrates how the artist gives form to a sigh, infuses life into the dead –

An enormous snore – journalist wakes up, jumps to his feet.

PICASSO: (*As English journalist.*) Absolutely top-hole old boy. Enormously grateful. Emotionally and intellectually stimulating!

Byee!

SABARTÉS: Satisfied?

PICASSO: You do *write* bullshit, Jaime.

SABARTÉS: The bull shits Pablo. Regularly.

PICASSO: Now... What....is...a woman?

SABARTÉS: (*In Lecturer mode.*) 'For Picasso, woman is shape, colour, and line, worthy of observation, just like any other object that he might study – '

PICASSO: Women?!!

Hah!

Every time I change women, I should burn the last one.

That way I'd be rid of her. She wouldn't be around to complicate my existence.

It would bring back my youth too!

Kill the woman and then you eradicate the past that she represents!

SABARTÉS: (*A beat, then, innocently.*) And what about Françoise?

PICASSO: (*A swift grin to audience.*) *I'll* become Françoise.

I want to play with her!

Lighting change. With prop doorknocker mounted on a piece of wood, he runs to imaginary door and knocks. SABARTÉS shuffles forward and opens door. During the following a few chairs can be used to chart the geography of the PICASSO household.

(As Françoise. Assumes carriage, walk and accent of a young French woman. Eagerly.) You must be Monsieur Sabartés. I'm Françoise Gilot.

SABARTÉS: Do you have an appointment?

PICASSO: *(As Françoise.)* Of course I do.

SABARTÉS: *(Peering around from behind glasses.)* Follow me if you please.

PICASSO: *(As Françoise.)* That's the spiky plant in the Dora Maar portrait, isn't it?

Last month: in the Louise Leiris Gallery!

Reacting with undisguised admiration to a painting on the wall.

Oh look at that! What a beautiful Matisse!

SABARTÉS: *(Turning around. Frostily.)* Here, there is only Picasso…

And here is the 'only' Picasso.

(Playing the game with a vengeance.) I'll become you, Pablo!

PICASSO: *(Squawks. As himself.)* Wha –

SABARTÉS: *(As PICASSO, playing him as a lecherous old man.)* Would you like me to show you around, my dear? You may *leave* Sabartés. I'll take over now!

PICASSO: *(As Françoise.)* Would you show me some of your paintings, Monsieur Picasso?

SABARTÉS: *(As PICASSO.)* Certainly my dear. We'll go downstairs first.

This is the sculpture studio. It was here, in this room, that I painted *Guernica*.

Hardly ever work here though.

(*Pointing.*) Except for *The Man with a Sheep.*

Now. Up again, through the big studio and: this is the bathroom.

I do my engraving here. See this?

(*Turns on a tap.*) Marvellous, isn't it? In spite of the war I have *hot* water!

PICASSO: (*As Françoise.*) That is truly astonishing, Monsieur.

SABARTÉS: (*As PICASSO.*) You could come up here…and have a nice hot bath any time you liked… Nice…hot…steamy water…

PICASSO: (*As Françoise. Hastily.*) You make your own resin, Monsieur Picasso?

SABARTÉS: (*As PICASSO. Grinning.*) Naturally. I'll show you some time.

Now. In here I think. You wanted to see some work of mine, didn't you?

Well Françoise, (*Turns over a canvas.*) what do you think of this one?

A nice big huge cock…crowing lustily!

Do you like cocks Françoise?

Françoise's hand goes to her mouth.

One should always paint what one knows…likes… Remember that.

(*Staring at her.*)

You need to strip off old habits; mentally undress the subject until you have only its bare essence.

PICASSO: (*As Françoise.*) I'm an artist too, Monsieur Picasso. A painter.

SABARTÉS: (*As PICASSO.*) Girls who look like you can't be painters!

PICASSO: *(As Françoise.)* Then perhaps you should look at my work in the gallery.

Rue Boissy d'Anglas...

(*Stroking her hair.*) Such lovely hair.

'PICASSO' cups his hands around her breasts. She doesn't react. He withdraws them in exasperation. Then suddenly he bends down and kisses her full on the mouth.

She just lets him.

SABARTÉS: (*As PICASSO. In surprise.*) You don't mind?

PICASSO: (*As Françoise.*) No. Should I?

SABARTÉS: (*As PICASSO.*) That's disgusting!

At least you could have pushed me away.

PICASSO: (*As Françoise.*) I'm at your disposition.

SABARTÉS: (*As PICASSO. A sudden intensity.*) Are you in love with me?

PICASSO: (*As Françoise.*) Oh I couldn't guarantee that. But I do like you.

SABARTÉS: (*As PICASSO: exasperated beyond measure.*) How do you expect me to seduce anyone under conditions like that? If you're not going to resist well...it's out of the question...

Beat: Lighting change. PICASSO swiftly changes the game and becomes the schoolgirl Geneviève Laporte, complete with schoolgirl voice and deportment. Knocks on door with a doorknocker. SABARTÉS is sitting at a table, filing documents, occasionally reading them. He has no intention of opening the door. But Geneviève is very persistent.

No callers please. (*Knocking.*) We are not receiving callers now.

(*Knocking.*) Nobody here. (*Knocking.*) Left Bank Brothel. (*Door opens.*)

PICASSO: (*As Laporte.*) Monsieur Picasso? (*Steps through.*)

I am a schoolgirl, a member of the F.N.E...

My name is Geneviève Laporte and I have come to interview you for my school magazine.

SABARTÉS: (*A momentary flicker of pleasure before.*) I am not Picasso. (*Laporte retreats.*)

But come back tomorrow and you'll see him.

PICASSO: (*As himself.*) You liked her, Geneviève, didn't you.

SABARTÉS: Maybe.

PICASSO: Could almost have been your daughter.

One hell of a fuck.

SABARTÉS: Doubtless.

PICASSO: Yes.

She became just like a daughter to you.

The three of you, sitting in your apartment: you, your wife. And young Geneviève. Translating your books.

Did you give her one Jaime?

SABARTÉS: Fuck off Picasso.

Strides off, mimes acquiring groceries, returns with a bag of them. We hear the ticking of a clock (or PICASSO makes the ticking sound). The hallmark of this sequence is a quiet understated domesticity. Mercedes is a constant but undemonstrative presence.

I'm back Mercedes, I'm back.

Takes off coat. Carefully puts it on hangar. Hangs it up.

Onion. Garlic. Chives. Raddish. Pate. Baguette.

Dos platos. Dos chios. Dos tenedores...

PICASSO enters as Mercedes. In the midst of the orderly rhythm of the laying out of the materials for lunch, SABARTÉS proffers one cheek, then the other for the routine greeting, and outlines his timetable

I have a meeting with Kahnweiler at four: publishing contract. Head of MOMA, New York, for dinner at seven. *He* chooses the restaurant.

Oh so frenchified is our American Monsieur.

He holds out his hands for Mercedes to wind on wool.

I will not be late.

Do we need –

PICASSO: (*As Mercedes.*) She's not taking lunch with us, Mademoiselle Laporte?

SABARTÉS: Geneviève never eats lunch, Mercedes. You know that.

PICASSO: (*As Mercedes.*) You shouldn't allow it Jaimes.

A growing girl needs to eat lunch. It's bad for her if she doesn't. You know that Jaimes.

You shouldn't allow it.

SABARTÉS: You know best. But we'll let Geneviève decide, shall we?

PICASSO: (*As Mercedes.*) Of course.

Jaimes is preparing lunch for us Genevieve…oh…

Mais oui, c'est ca… (*Finishes wool-winding.*)

SABARTÉS: (*Coming over.*) We can work over here
Geneviève.

*He sits at a table, opens books etc. PICASSO as Mercedes, sits
beside a window and starts to knit, occasionally humming or
crooning to herself.*

Hmmm? (*Laughs.*) Yes…I suppose I'm not the easiest to
translate into French. Keep using Catalan argot.

Yes! Pre 1900!

Looking to wall in response to her glance.

That was painted in 1941.

Which print? Ah! (*Going over.*) You can see the
inscription: 'To Jaimes Sabartés, the only musketeer.
From his *malagueno ami*, Picasso'.

Music, possibly Albeniz, bathed in the glow of memory.

Oh yes. All the time. When I was about your age
(*Glances at Mercedes.*) in and out of *Els Quatre Gats*,
drinking coffee laced with flaming rum, going down to
the brothels in the sailors' quarters…

Pablo always liked the brothels…

In and out, out and in, no cares, then straight to work.

I'd often just wait on him, chatting to the girls…

Pablo was more…ah…active than I was…

Some beautiful girls…as slender, as elegant, as…poised
as yourself.

(*Almost bashful.*) If we had been graced with a daughter, I'd like to think that she would have looked…just like them…slender, elegant, oh so poised, calm, quiet…comfortable…

Mercedes? Oh… She was my childhood sweetheart, even when I was elsewhere…even when I was elsewhere.

(*Returns to Geneviève.*) Now where were we…ah…yes…

Music ends.

PICASSO: (*As Mercedes.*) Jaime…

SABARTÉS: Yes, my love…

PICASSO: (*As Mercedes. Smiling.*) It's nice to have you back…

SABARTÉS: It's nice to be back…

PICASSO: (*As Mercedes.*) Si.

SABARTÉS: Si. (*To Geneviève.*) Let us continue…

Snapping out of this and driving into the following without a beat.

PICASSO: They're making wars just to annoy me. Why didn't they tell me? It's taking things just a bit too far! Don't you think it's fate?

SABARTÉS: No.

PICASSO: First Vollard, ensconced in the back of his car, driving along.

Seizes two chairs and uses them, back to back, as cars.

Two cars: bumph!

And what happens?

He's killed by a bronze that's been sitting in the rear window!

SABARTÉS is already using four chairs to imprison PICASSO inside a small space. PICASSO sinks down into it, his head poking out nervously and looking around.

And now, just as I'm beginning to *do* some work, France goes to war!

SABARTÉS snapping into being a German officer: walking ominously along the platforms of the chairs.

This is where Herr Lipchitz lives, isn't it?

Monsieur Lipchitz is in America.

This is Monsieur Picasso's apartment.

SABARTÉS: (*As German officer.*) Oh no…

We know it's Herr Lipchitz's apartment.

PICASSO: But no. (*Insisting.*) This is the house of Monsieur Picasso.

SABARTÉS: (*As German.*) Monsieur Picasso isn't a Jew by any chance?

PICASSO: Of course not!

SABARTÉS: (*As German.*) We would like to be sure.

We will search for papers.

PICASSO: (*Coming out from the chairs and playing off the audience.*) The thing about the Germans is…well…

I didn't want to leave Paris, did I? Why should I?

I wasn't French, was I?

So –

SABARTÉS: So you made sure that you had powerful friends. A little oiling here and there…selling canvases to dealers who worked with the Nazis…

(*A beat. To audience.*) We are in the only heated room of the studio in Rue des Grands Augustins.

Chairs are arranged, as if around a table.

I had arrived to find Marcel, the chauffeur, chewing his lips.

Inez, the housekeeper: her mischievous smile. No longer there.

Instead, that face and body, regarded by others as eloquent and pneumatique, is taut and strained.

(*Pointing to PICASSO.*) He scarcely acknowledges me.

We are gathered around the table like a funeral party around a bier.

PICASSO: (*Eyes flashing: the Grand Inquisitor.*) Where is it? My little pocket flashlight.

I left it here. Right here. On this chair.

And it isn't here now!

SABARTÉS: (*To audience.*) Quel surprise! Oh la la...

PICASSO: If it isn't here now, then somebody had to take it. Marcel? Inez? Jaime?

I spent the entire night looking for it!

I will not tol-er-ate things disappearing in my house.

I demand, absolutely demand, that it be found.

At once! (*Stalks off.*)

SABARTÉS: (*Casually, to audience.*) He did it himself. Unquestioningly. Must have put it somewhere and forgotten. So he accuses everyone else.

Typical!

(*To audience.*) Another day.

(*Showing us where the servants are.*) Marcel. Inez.

If Baron Mollet arrives, tell him that Picasso has gone out.

If the American woman comes, shut her in the studio so that she won't see him.

If the publisher presents himself, announce *him* straightaway.

(*To audience.*) Bloody Americans. They're all the same. She's coming here just so she can tell her friends in New York that, in Europe, she saw the Pope, The Escorial, Pompeii, Versailles, and Pablo Picasso.

Another day.

Brassai is in the studio, still photographing sculpture. Pablo, true to form, has retired there as well, but not to work. He's escaping the crowd who are waiting patiently below.

Goes across to studio.

PICASSO: Why can't they leave me in peace?

SABARTÉS: You'd be screaming with rage if no one came. Everyone's deserted you, you'd say.

Nobody loves you!

PICASSO: Don't be ridiculous.

SABARTÉS: It's your system. Appointments until one. Open day: Saturday morning.

PICASSO: You are supposed to vet matters. Why else do I pay you?

SABARTÉS: (*Patiently.*) They are waiting for you. They have been waiting for over two hours.

PICASSO: I'm ill! My sister's just broken her leg.

SABARTÉS: She's dead. You're not.

PICASSO: Tell them I'm at Lacourière's, checking plate proofs.

SABARTÉS: (*Pushing PICASSO towards the door, like a director with a recalcitrant actor who has stage fright.*) It's too late now. We've made them wait too long.

They know you're here.

PICASSO: All right, all right. I'm going. (*Runs comb through his hair. Takes a deep breath.*) I'm going.

SABARTÉS: (*To audience.*) Just like a woman.

PICASSO: Hah! What about yourself? (*He's thinking: two can play at this game.*)

(*As Françoise.*) You've come to photograph all of the sculptures, Monsieur Brassai?

SABARTÉS: (*To Françoise: with an edge.*) Françoise. It's nobody's business why he's here, what he's doing, or how long he stays.

PICASSO: (*As Françoise.*) I've known Brassai for longer than I've known Pablo!

SABARTÉS: Then see him outside and ask him there!

(*Snapping out of it. To audience.*) You think I'm awkward? You know what he did to Maillol?

For an extra 'edge' the following sequence can be played as if Maillol is somewhat deaf. Although in his eighties, Maillol is still capable of making sculpture. He is frail but resilient. Music: perhaps a touch of Catalan folk music.

PICASSO: (*To audience.*) That bugger Maillol. Bloody Catalan. Lousy sculptor.

SABARTÉS: (*As Maillol.*) Monsieur Picasso! Such an honour!

PICASSO: I did come out to see you once before.

Here. To Ville-Neuve Saint Georges.

Sang you a Catalan song!

SABARTÉS: (*As Maillol.*) You were twenty when you arrived from Spain. Slim.

An intelligent face. Looked like a girl.

PICASSO: (*To audience, referring to Maillol.*) Soon be dead!

SABARTÉS: (*As Maillol, referring to PICASSO. To audience.*) Now he's grown thick. Face like a toad.

(*To PICASSO.*) You're very welcome.

PICASSO: (*With grave courtesy.*) Thank you.

(*Nonchalantly.*) Van Dongen here? I just need him to –

SABARTÉS: (*As Maillol. To audience.*) He just needed Van Dongen to work for him.

(*To PICASSO.*) Van Dongen is my assistant.

Never mind Picasso. You honour me with your presence.

Have a look at this sculpture: I have a problem. Here.

You see?

Tell me what you think. Honestly.

PICASSO turns and stalks off.

Beat.

Do you call that an artist!!

Do you think Michangelo would have turned his back if I'd asked for advice?

Of course not. He'd have picked up his chisel and shown me what to do!

Snapping out of it. To audience.

(*As SABARTÉS.*) He was just as arrogant with the literary world.

PICASSO: You've read my poetry Gertrude?

Verve are going to publish it. Andre Breton loves it.

Going to write an essay on it!

SABARTÉS: (*As Gertrude Stein, complete with accent.*) Really?

PICASSO: (*Butter not melting in his mouth.*) Yes…!

SABARTÉS: (*As Stein.*) You can't stand looking at Jean Cocteau's drawings, can you Pablo?

For you they're more offensive than just bad drawings. Just so?

Well, for me, that's the way it is with your poetry.

You never read a book in your life that wasn't written by a friend.

Words annoy you, more than they do anything else – so how can you write?

PICASSO: (*Truculently.*) You always said I was an extraordinary person.

SABARTÉS: (*As Stein. Taking him by the lapels and shaking him.*) You are extraordinary. Within your limits.

PICASSO: So. Supposing I know it, what will I do?

SABARTÉS: (*As Stein.*) You will continue until you are in a more cheerful disposition, and then you will paint a very beautiful picture, and then more of them.

PICASSO: Yes.

Gertrude walks off.

(*To audience.*) Talent?

Gertrude had the talent to recognize me for what I was: a genius. But Gertrude herself? No talent.

Big ego but no talent. She thinks she discovered me. Hah!

I discovered myself.

(*Without a beat.*) Now Eva. There was a woman! One I truly loved.

SABARTÉS: Bullsh –

PICASSO: Listen Sabartés. You weren't there. You were in South America, remember?

I was.

So I know.

SABARTÉS: But I have access to other information...now...

PICASSO: Your job, friend, was to create the myth.

If you weren't there, then I did it, or I got someone else to do it for me.

And the myth – the truth – is that I loved Eva.

With her, there was no-one else.

SABARTÉS: (*Mimicking.*) 'With her there was no-one else'.

(*As music-hall routine.*) What's it like to be dead Eva?

Deadly Jaimes.

What was he like in the sack, Eva?

Bloody awful. Deadly boring and –

PICASSO: Bollocks!

(*Utterly outraged.*) *No one* ever said that about me!

SABARTÉS: Dearie me.

You want me to tell the truth, eh?

Let's see now. Ah!

'Picasso's second major love, Marcelle Humbert, was rechristened Eva by the painter, as a declaration that he was Adam and she was the first woman, the only woman, Eva.'

PICASSO: Exactly.

SABARTÉS: Truth is a rather flexible commodity.

Marcelle Humbert was *born* Eva Gouel.

The only reason you returned to her baptismal name was –

PICASSO: Have it your own way.

I am, as usual, correct.

SABARTÉS: Did she make any contribution to your art?

PICASSO: Don't be ridiculous.

SABARTÉS: Nineteen thirteen, nineteen fourteen and nineteen fifteen… (*Clicks his fingers.*)

You're Eva. I'm Georges Braque.

Lighting change. As Braque. A Normandy Man. Tall, muscular, rather deliberate of voice and character.

(*With courtesy.*) You like our *ragoût?*

PICASSO: (*As Eva. Petite, delicate and perfect. Donning a kimono.*) I've never known Pablo to cook before.

You would obviously make him an excellent wife…

She begins to cough.

SABARTÉS: (*As Braque.*) You need to get that man to take care of you. Have you seen a doctor?

PICASSO: (*As Eva, swiftly.*) I'm not ill. It's just a cough and –

SABARTÉS: (*As Braque.*) Pablo can't stand anyone being ill.

PICASSO: (*As Eva.*) He takes it as a personal injustice…as if it's a deliberate attempt to annoy him…

SABARTÉS: (*As Braque.*) Very Spanish!

PICASSO: (*As Eva.*) It's not that he doesn't love me…

It disturbs his work…his concentration, and –

SABARTÉS: (*As Braque.*) And he's obsessive.

I'm obsessive about painting. Pablo's obsessive about everything!

PICASSO: (*Starting to take off kimono – as PICASSO.*) I've had enough of this manipulation –

SABARTÉS: (*As himself.*) Stay!

Beat. PICASSO unwillingly becomes Eva again.

Mademoiselle Eva. Please excuse this interruption.

I'm a friend of Picasso's…from his student days. I'm writing a book on him. Would you mind if I interviewed you?

PICASSO: (*Venomously starting to take off kimono again.*) Piss off you wee homunculus, I'll –

SABARTÉS: You'll – do – what – you're – told.

Beat. PICASSO tries to resist and finds that he cannot. Becomes Eva.

Monsieur Jaime Sabartés. But please call me Jaime.

PICASSO: (*As Eva.*) To tell you the truth, Pablo's so busy that most of the time I'm on my own and there's not much to do here in the suburbs.

He's a very important artist, isn't he?

SABARTÉS: Yes. I think he is.

Do you ever help him with his work?

PICASSO: (*As Eva. Laughing.*) Oh no! How could I help an artist! I can organise for him, meet clients, ensure that his finances are tended carefully.

I suppose I do talk to him about his work.

He was having problems with a sculpture he was making. A cubist version of a guitar, so I was able to solve some practical problems for him. I make my own dresses you see. Know all about patterns, positioning, how to relate two dimensions to a three-dimensional object. I even suggested he use dressmaker's pins – and he did.

But that's not really helping with his work, is it?

SABARTÉS: Have you been ill for long?

PICASSO: (*As Eva. Nervously.*) Ill?

SABARTÉS: Your cough. You think it's angina?

PICASSO: (*As Eva.*) Don't tell Pablo! He hates illness.

SABARTÉS: (*To audience.*) Nineteen fourteen.

(*To Eva.*) Your cough. You think it's tuberculosis?

PICASSO: (*As Eva.*) Pablo smokes a pipe. A big English one. I think he hopes the smoke will protect him…

I'm frightened.

SABARTÉS: (*To audience.*) Nineteen fifteen.

(*To Eva.*) You like the sanatorium?

PICASSO: (*As Eva.*) Cancer. I'm dying. He'll never marry me now, will he?

(*Brightly.*) He comes every day. All the way across town on the metro. It eats up into the time he has for his work...but he still comes...

He's a good man...

SABARTÉS clicks his fingers.

PICASSO: (*Tearing off kimono.*) I'm a good man, right?

SABARTÉS: Nineteen fifteen. I'll be Eva.

Split-stage effect. PABLO finds himself catapulted into his earlier self.

PICASSO: Take off your clothes, Gaby, my love –

SABARTÉS: (*As Eva.*) Doctor! Is there...?

Oh...

PICASSO: (*Unzipping.*) Open your legs my love and I'll make us both immortal!

SABARTÉS: (*As Eva.*) A few months...a few months...

PICASSO: (*Thrusting energetically.*) Now that, Gaby, (*As he comes.*) is what I call a good fuck!

SABARTÉS: (*As Eva.*) Pablo, where are you my love? Don't leave me...please...Pablo...where are you...

PICASSO: (*Zipping up his flies.*) We'll go off to the country for a few days...

Enjoy ourselves. Okay?

SABARTÉS: Dies, in considerable pain, December 1915. Well?

PICASSO: I hadn't had sex for months.

What the hell did you expect me to do? Become a monk?

SABARTÉS: (*Beat.*) Promise and fulfilment.

(*To audience.*) Two things which rarely coincide with him.

PICASSO: (*Rubbing it in.*) Geniuses make their own rules, don't they?

Music: Debussy's L'Apres Midi d'un Faun plays softly.

SABARTÉS: (*To audience.*) The Rue La Boetie. A family. Marcel the chauffeur. Inez the maid.

My wife Mercedes: the housekeeper.

Current mistress: Dora…

If you have a dining-room table, naturally you clear it for a meal. With Pablo a table was a space to be filled: a pocket book, a diary, a filing-system, only one organised to a set of rules that only he understood. So, naturally, the dining table lost its proper function, much to the annoyance of Mercedes.

(*Pointing.*) Mantelpiece, a marble-topped buffet, chairs, an old radio, an armchair, the stuffing of which oozed out like sap; a sofa, oozing like puss…it was a minefield…an exercise for cadets in army initiative. Could they navigate the room without detonating Pablo's temper by even minutely disturbing the volcanic lava of books, letters, *disques bleus*, newspapers, matches, electric lamps, postcards, castanets, boxes, shells, small rocks, nails, keys, pocket-knives, razors, cigarette-lighters, ribbons, erasers, pencils, bottles, banknotes in wonderful and weird currencies, sculptures, flags, pompoms, corks, bits of bone…

Believe it!

PICASSO: (*To audience.*) You know the way women are. They want to clean and tidy and dust and bugger up everything! She ruined my system. Kept trying to put me into little compartments. So I exploded! Tough.

SABARTÉS: 1937.

Myself, and Mercedes had to leave this apartment.

Dora…oh yes…women…

Dora didn't like me, she wanted me out of the way…

And she got her way.

All right for Pablo.

What was money to him except that he didn't like spending it?

But for me, I needed money for an apartment. A cheap apartment.

Fourteenth arrondisement. Rue Jean-Dolent.

Which also meant that we needed money for travel, for additional meals, for furnishings.

All very well for Pablo.

I had to ring, and we would have to wait, like beggars, to get into the Picasso residence…just like everyone else.

Monsieur Picasso! Monsieur Picasso!

A few weeks later, he told me to get out.

For good.

And I did.

(*Venomously.*) Who did he think he was?

Well, I told them. I told anyone who would listen.

I told them that Picasso beat his women, that he let his mother go hungry, that he was an aggressive, rapacious, malicious, vindictive old bastard.

PICASSO: (*To audience.*) An overheated imagination.

It happened like this.

(*To SABARTÉS, before he can interject.*) I'll play Mercedes!

(*As Mercedes, playing her like a tease in a French farce.*) Jaime has gone out on an errand for you, hasn't he?

SABARTÉS: (*As PICASSO.*) Yes.

PICASSO: (*As Mercedes.*) Would you like me to do anything for you?

SABARTÉS: (*As PICASSO. Beat.*) Anything?

PICASSO: (*As Mercedes: innocently. Bending over the table to dust and display her rump.*) Jaime told me to help you in any way I could Monsieur.

SABARTÉS: (*As PICASSO.*) Did he indeed?

PICASSO: (*As Mercedes: very innocently.*) Why yes Monsieur…

SABARTÉS: (*As PICASSO.*) Wouldn't want to disappoint him now, would we?

PICASSO: (*As Mercedes.*) Oh no Monsieur…

SABARTÉS: (*As PICASSO: coming over to her.*) I've a bad back. Difficult to bend.

Could you undo my belt buckle? (*She does so.*)

Very constricting these trousers, could you lower them?

(*Does so.*)

There's something on the floor there, I think. (*She kneels in front of him.*)

One needs gentleness, no? (*She pulls down his underpants.*) Do you think you could help me Mercedes?

PICASSO: (*As Mercedes.*) Why yes Monsieur. It would be a pleasure.

As 'she' starts to 'fellate' him, SABARTÉS breaks out of the game violently.

SABARTÉS: Bastard! It happened like this.

For a second they confront each other like boxers. Then PICASSO grins and enters the game.

PICASSO: (*Artlessly.*) Mercedes! Mercedes!

SABARTÉS: (*As Mercedes: her normal self.*) Yes Monsieur Picasso? Jaime is away on an errand for you.

PICASSO: Could you get me that book over there Mercedes?

SABARTÉS: (*As Mercedes.*) At the far end of the table?

PICASSO: That's right.

Mercedes bends over the table, her rump in the air. PICASSO comes up behind her. His hands run up her legs, caress her bottom.

I'm really fond of Jaime…but you know that, don't you Mercedes. We share everything. Everything.

Always have.

Oh I know he's not great in the cunt-fuck department…never was…but it doesn't really matter.

I'm more than sufficient for all of us.

He is rubbing himself against her, fillups up her dress, takes down her stockings etc. Hands around her breasts. Inserts himself.

Don't you worry. I'll not tell him. It'll be our little secret. We can do it every day. Twice a day if you like. Any position.

Jesus, you're one hell of a shag Mercedes.

(*Beginning to come.*) One – hell – of – a (*Screaming.*) – SHAG!

Rolls off, exhausted and lies on the ground.

SABARTÉS: (*As Mercedes. Puts on her clothes. The victim. Utterly withdrawn.*) I'll go now Monsieur Picasso. Jaime might be back.

I love Jaime.

(*As part of the game. To PICASSO. With intensity.*) I love him.

I *love* him…

A long long beat during which the music stops, then, venomously.

You bastard. That was my wife!

PICASSO: (*Pleasantly.*) Pure fantasy!

Besides. With a man like Picasso, it wouldn't have been rape.

Would it?

End of Act One.

ACT TWO

PICASSO: What was it I said? Ah! (*Clicks fingers. A drumroll.*) 'It wouldn't have been rape, would it?'

(*Beat.*) You came back to me.

Didn't you?

SABARTÉS: (*Coldly. To audience.*) For one whole year I never saw him. We went hungry that year. I had to start writing journalism again.

I walked everywhere.

Music: Café Concert style music used to punctuate the Park sequence.

April the seventh. 2:16 pm. The park in Saint-Germain-des-Prés. I was walking through.

PICASSO: (*Running over with dog on leash.*) Sabartés! Jaime Sabartés! You're such an awful man Jaime. You never come round to see me anymore!

(*Before SABARTÉS can get a word in edgeways.*) Come along with me. I'll show you my new studio. Great space. Not that far from here. Just wait 'til you see it, I'll –

SABARTÉS: I'm busy. Really busy. Another time.

PICASSO: Rue des Grand Augustins. 7 Rue des Grand Augustins. You'll remember that, 7 –

SABARTÉS: Rue des Grand Augustins.

PICASSO: (*To audience.*) Seven weeks passed. The bugger never came. Naturally I walked my dog in the park: same day, same time, every week.

Naturally, we met again.

Sabartés! Old friend! Jaime! The only real friend I've ever had! You're such an awful man Jaime. You never come round to see me any more. Come along with me. I'll show you my new studio. Great space. Not that far from here. 7 –

SABARTÉS: Rue des Grands Augustins?

PICASSO: Why yes. You've heard of it?

SABARTÉS: No.

That's where that cafe is. Whatchamaycallit?

PICASSO: The Ulanova?

SABARTÉS: Maybe. Anyway. I'm busy. Very busy. See ya!

PICASSO: (*To audience.*) Lying wee bastard!

You'd think I was being unreasonable, wouldn't you!

I sent him a letter.

SABARTÉS: (*Producing letter with a flourish.*) See? This letter. Pablo Picasso, the great Pablo Picasso, sent me, me, this letter. See that? Written in crayon.

In seven different colours!

'My dearest friend Sabartés, you promised me that you would come to see me. I know you don't like meeting other people, so you could come secretly.

Your old friend Paco Durio is coming to see me on Thursday the fifth of July at three forty-five pm. And he wants very much to see you. As do I.

Write to me here. With much love, I remain, your faithful servant, Pablo Picasso'

PICASSO: (*To audience.*) Clever, eh?

Did the trick.

Sabartés! My old friend. Now you see these poems of mine, I need you to transcribe them, translate them, put them in order –

SABARTÉS: I've already done that!

PICASSO: Ah! But this time, you'll do it even better. Just like the old times.

The two musketeers. Us. Whatcha say?

SABARTÉS: (*To audience.*) Why are you lot looking so smug?

I left him, didn't I?

So I go back…

Look, there could have been all sorts of reasons for me to leave.

PICASSO: There were.

SABARTÉS: He was trying to get a divorce from Olga. She didn't want one, and I was summoned to appear…on her side.

Traitor, he called me. Me…a traitor!

Could I help it if I was ordered to appear?

PICASSO: Actually the problem was Mercedes. Living with Jaime: no problem. But someone whom I couldn't tell to fuck off whenever I felt like it, now *that* was a problem.

Lighting change. A touch of percussive music.

What…is a woman?

SABARTÉS: (*To audience.*) 'For Picasso, woman is shape, colour, and line, worthy of observation, just like any other *object* that he might study – '

PICASSO: (*Grins to the audience, then.*) He's repeating himself.

Suddenly going on the offensive.

Did you dream –

SABARTÉS: No –

PICASSO: Did you dream of yourself as the Minotaur –

SABARTÉS: No –

PICASSO: Did you dream of yourself, satiated and sleek, ripening in the sunshine that slants through the window –

SABARTÉS: No –

PICASSO: – Black, horned, bull-like, the soft sheets sliding over your powerful pawing body –

SABARTÉS: Piss off!

PICASSO: Your black pelt quickened and stoked into passion as the thick folding curves of a body – Is it Fernande? – unsheath themselves to your pawing breath –

SABARTÉS: (*Deliberately.*) Piss Artist.

PICASSO: You turn your head – Is it Dora? – whose imperious nakedness is displayed in a rhythm of orifice and breast... Now the face and the form deliquesce, hazing into the ample, succulent and yielding shape of a Marie-Thèrèse...

A naked ballerina glides through the mirror of the room –

SABARTÉS: Having a wet dream, are we?

PICASSO: A choir of nymphets, naked and nurturing, billow their blossoming voices around your ears and –

SABARTÉS: It's *el decadente Picasso,* the posing poet, symbol-stuffed! You – are – watching – yourself!

Guarding sleep! Those waking dreams your imprimatur, your licence to lust, your confirmation that the waking world is simply seeping from your head, made manifest in the creamy cavities of a sketchbook page.

PICASSO: You do *write* bullshit, Jaime.

SABARTÉS: (*To audience.*) He's repeating himself!

(*Deadpan.*) The bull shits Pablo. Regularly.

PICASSO: You could take up a new career Jaime. The Academic. 'Sex and Surrealism: the function of Pablo Picasso's lavatory paper'.

SABARTÉS: You could play at a new game, Pablo. 'The artist as concerned citizen!' 'Women, as the guiding moral and spiritual light!'

PICASSO: Women?!! Guiding? Me!

(*Beat.*) Women are either Goddesses or doormats.

Men are either dickheads, or they can be used: in the service of the work.

SABARTÉS: What did the artist *offer*, especially to women? Wasn't it the promise of immortality?

PICASSO: (*Nipping in.*) And sex –

SABARTÉS: (*Relentlessly.*) Access to the aphrodisiac of power, fame, fortune –

PICASSO: Sex and money: I told you. Pure combustion! Everything I touch turns to gold. Midas, right?

But those close to me, flying too close to the sun, they burn up, like Icarus!

(*Makes a falling sound.*) Drop like a stone and drown! 'Picasso and Erudition!'

(*As an afterthought.*) Hemingway left a crate of handgrenades for me! In Paris.

Liberation!

SABARTÉS: (*Undeterred. To audience.*) Pablo Ruiz Picasso is a cynical torturer. He demands uncritical adulation and –

PICASSO: (*Brushing him off like a fly.*) – everybody takes advantage of me. Everybody. They all want something. So I pay in kind.

And I write my autobiography in every drawing, sculpture, painting, ceramic, and print that I make –

So look at the work Sabartés: the biography is irrelevant.

I am what I made.

There is no other reason for life.

Everything – everything Sabartés – is a precondition for work. Nothing exists outside of work.

Every waking glance, every shard of the surreal dream, every fuck, every jism of an erotic daydream, every casual conversation, every trawl along a street or a shoreline, every garbage bin, movie, flick through a book, every billboard glimpsed from a car, every unexpected guest – all of it – sex, people, information, stimulation, it's just fuel for the canvas, clay for the sculpture.

Do I use? What artist doesn't?

Do I misuse? The question is irrelevant.

I leave something behind.

If nobody has any real importance for me, that's because everyone has some importance for me.

I take what is useful. I discard what isn't.

That's called intelligence.

SABARTÉS: Apollinaire. Fernande. Max Jacob. Olga –

PICASSO: This is my credo so shut up.

People or things. What's the difference.

I give something back. Always.

How many people can say that?

I touch lives. I quicken people. I bring emotion, excitement, adrenalin.

And I offer my own version of eternity.

Only God can equal that!

So I make a fiction! So I use you to create a legend!

So what?

I lie into truth.

SABARTÉS: Got that off our chest, have we?

Now we play my game so *you* – shut up!

Lights! Music! Drumroll!

Music: fanfare and drumroll.

And now, ladies and gentlemen, as your substitute for sex, power and domination, I give you the one absolute ritual of the Picasso day: the *lévee*.

(*Deadpan.*) Subtitled: Getting Pablo Up.

Clicks his fingers. PICASSO springs into action. Four lines of string criss-cross the stage at PICASSO's head height. Each is festooned with letters, held by clothespegs. SABARTÉS, who is taller, (as are most other people) has acquired a kind of loping, ducking-and-diving when he is transversing the room. PICASSO slides into bed and becomes comatose, surrounded as ever, by huge piles of books, cigarette cartons, etcetera. The following scene is briskly paced. Music can be used to signal each of the 'military manoeuvres' that SABARTÉS uses.

63

SABARTÉS: (*Walking over and picking up envelope.*) Pablo of course has been on one of his nightly excursions to the cafes.

Without me.

So he leaves me notes.

Lifts out handwritten note from envelope.

Shoved under my door. Usually in an old envelope. Keeps expenses down.

PICASSO: 'Jaime. It is now two-thirty am on the eleventh of February, nineteen thirty six'.

SABARTÉS: (*To audience.*) He writes the date in roman numerals. Showing off.

PICASSO: 'Leap into my room at eight-thirty and wake me up'. Pablo.

SABARTÉS: Hah.

If I did that, he'd go beserk!

Military fanfare.

Ten forty-five. Military tactic number one. Send in Inez, the chambermaid! With breakfast.

(*As he becomes Inez.*) Like a chambermaid out of a french farce. Starched apron. Black stockings. Fine legs. Very pretty –and proud of her position in life: chambermaid to a great painter.

Shyly flirtatious. Runs in and out with short steps.

(*As Inez.*) Monsieur Picasso. Monsieur Picasso.

PICASSO: (*Without stirring.*) Go away.

SABARTÉS: (*As Inez.*) Monsieur Picasso. It is nearly eleven o'clock. You must eat Monsieur Picasso.

PICASSO's head emerges, blearily.

You must eat.

PICASSO: You're looking very pretty this morning Inez.

SABARTÉS: (*As Inez.*) Thank you Monsieur Picasso.

She bends forwards, placing tray on bed.

PICASSO: (*Eying her legs.*) Getting up is always so difficult…in the morning.

SABARTÉS: (*As Inez.*) Of course Monsieur.

PICASSO: (*Grumbling.*) It's not right.

SABARTÉS: (*As Inez.*) Two pieces of dried toast. Salt-free. *Café au lait.*

It is as usual Monsieur.

PICASSO: The toast is in the wrong place.

SABARTÉS: (*As Inez. Bends over and re-arranges it. PICASSO eyes her legs.*) There you are Monsieur. Is everything to your satisfaction? Thank you Monsieur.

She curtsies – PICASSO eyes her legs – and she exits.

(*As SABARTÉS: to audience.*) Like the brass bed?

Military fanfare.

Military tactic Number Two: the papers, and the mail.

Picks up a collection of both, then in he goes.

Morning Pablo. Newspapers (placing each one down): *Le Figaro, Le Journal* and *The Excelsior.* The clippings service. (*Puts down.*) Your mail. (*Placing each section down.*) Invitations. Sales catalogues. Letters.

PICASSO: What time is it?

SABARTÉS: Ten minutes past eleven.

PICASSO: (*Sips coffee. Flicks through letters, seizes on one.*) All these people. Do they think I've nothing better to do?

SABARTÉS: (*To audience.*) If they didn't write, he'd complain bitterly!

(*To PICASSO.*) They want contact with a genius.

PICASSO: What time is it?

SABARTÉS: Time to get up.

PICASSO: (*Looks under sheet, grins.*) I am up!

SABARTÉS: Time to get up.

PICASSO: What for?

SABARTÉS: *Mon vieux*: To take all of that anxiety and worry away from you.

PICASSO: Let's talk about something else.

What time is it?

SABARTÉS: Half past eleven.

PICASSO: (*Brandishing a letter.*) See! Olga yet again.

She torments me, that woman.

SABARTÉS: You don't have to read them.

PICASSO: Of course I have to read them. They're written to me, aren't they? I have to know what she says, don't I? Look at this. My son Paulo. In trouble – again!

What time is it?

SABARTÉS: Twelve o' clock.

Military fanfare.

(*To audience.*) Military tactic Number Three: Listen to the lamentations.

PICASSO: I'm a sick man. My stomach. It's probably cancer. I'm *dying*.

Nobody cares about me. Nobody.

(*Beat.*) Nobody.

SABARTÉS: We all care about you, young Picasso. The whole world cares about you. Isn't your every move reported in the newspapers?

PICASSO: Hah! What does the whole world care? The whole world wants tittle-tattle.

Who I slept with last night.

How much money my last painting made at auction!

That's not caring.

SABARTÉS: (*Deadpan.*) Oh. I see. You want the whole world to love you.

PICASSO: What time is it?

SABARTÉS: Twenty past twelve. You're not sick. Your doctor is enormously fond of you –

PICASSO: Well he doesn't come round every day, does he!

SABARTÉS: Doctors only come round every day to patients who are seriously ill.

PICASSO: I am ill. Seriously. (*Tragically.*) I'm *dying*.

(*Looks out of the corner of his eye: no response.*) He's a useless doctor. He's an incompetent.

He told me I could drink whiskey. On *my* stomach!

What kind of a doctor would tell you to do a thing like that?

Military fanfare.

SABARTÉS: (*To audience.*) Military Manoeuvre Number Four: arselicking.

(*To PICASSO.*) You're alive. So far as I can tell. Everybody loves you, even me.

And what's more, what's absolutely, definitely more, is that your latest work is superb!

PICASSO: Really?

SABARTÉS: Yes.

PICASSO: That's true. But are *you* sure?

SABARTÉS: On the lives of my children.

PICASSO: You haven't got any children. Now.

SABARTÉS: On the lives of my wife, myself, yourself –

PICASSO: (*In horror.*) You can't say that!

SABARTÉS: What?

PICASSO: On my life! It's bad luck.

SABARTÉS: Rubbish. There's no such superstition.

PICASSO: Yes there is.

SABARTÉS: (*Suspiciously.*) I never heard it.

PICASSO: My uncles! Yes, it was one of my uncles. Uncle Rodrigo –

SABARTÉS: You don't have an uncle Rodrigo –

PICASSO: Yes I do.

SABARTÉS: I'm your biographer, and you never told me!

PICASSO: Well I'm telling you now! And Uncle Rodrigo always said that if someone swore on your own life, then you die within three weeks unless...

SABARTÉS: (*Deeply suspicious.*) Unless what?

PICASSO: Unless you bless yourself with your left hand while turning clockwise, then turn anticlockwise while spitting.

SABARTÉS: You expect me to believe that?

PICASSO: (*Screaming.*) Do it! Do you want me to die!

SABARTÉS: Very well. (*Does so exactly, ending up with a spit at PICASSO.*) Satisfied?

PICASSO: More or less.

You're sure my latest work is superb?

SABARTÉS: Yes.

PICASSO: What time is it?

SABARTÉS: Ten minutes to one.

PICASSO: Ten minutes to one? Ten minutes to one?

What do you mean by letting me lie on until this time?

What do I pay you for? You're supposed to be my secretary.

To look after my interests.

Aren't there scores of people waiting for me in the vestibule?

SABARTÉS: Yes.

PICASSO: Well you're going to take the blame for keeping them waiting. It was your fault. Not getting me up in time. It most assuredly wasn't mine. (*Getting up.*)

SABARTÉS: Your clothes:

Baggy trousers.

Watch, dangling from lapel by a shoelace.

Torn pockets held together by safety pins.

A Basque beret for a balding head.

Ready, are we?

PICASSO: No thanks to you.

How long have those people been waiting? Two hours?
Three hours. It's disgusting.

Someone has to pay!

SABARTÉS: (*To audience.*) Guess who?

(*Beat.*) Why do I put up with him?

(*Clicks his fingers: we see an image of PICASSO's sculpture
The Goat, or a version of it projected onto a screen that
partially descends from the Gods. Points upwards.*) Watch a
miracle.

*Becomes Françoise. Finds, or mimes finding, a baby carriage.
The dump can be represented by a few upturned chairs. The
actions throughout the sequence can be mimed.*

PICASSO: I want to go for a walk.

SABARTÉS: Through the backstreets and past the dump?

PICASSO: Of course. One must make one's luck. Be
stimulated by the accidental.

They walk.

Why buy materials if you can get them for free?

SABARTÉS: You don't mean that.

PICASSO: A shape here, a memory there.

Picking up two bits of cardboard, tossing into baby carriage.

Shape them, fill with plaster, and I have ears!

Everything changes.

Anything can become art, if you have eyes, if you see the metaphor.

Ah! The dump!

Scrabbles around enthusiastically: holds up two broken milk pitchers.

SABARTÉS: They'll become?

PICASSO: I just like them. (*Places them lovingly in carriage, returns to dump.*)

SABARTÉS: (*To audience.*) The goat's udders!

PICASSO: Yes! (*Triumphantly holds up a broken wickerbasket.*) The goat's stomach. It's rib-cage, see? (*Tosses into carriage.*)

SABARTÉS: On the beach, he found a palm branch.

That became the backbone.

Another bit he carved for nose and mouth.

PICASSO: (*Brandishing a series of branches.*) Legs. See these ones with knots: hind-legs!

Finds bits of metal ribbing.

Stick 'em into the haunches: nice and bony and angular.

They start to walk off. He hesitates, spotting something else.

Ah! (*Grabs bit of tin can, bends it into two.*) Up the bum for the bollocks!

Goes off whistling.

SABARTÉS: (*As Françoise. As she trundles behind.*) A couple of bits of copper wire found in the street.

71

Twist together like a plait, and there's your tail.

Seems easy, doesn't it? Effortless…

He makes it seem so simple.

Pushes carriage back into 'dump'.

Of course everyone's doing it now.…aping the outside…

PICASSO: (*Calling over.*) I taught her all she knew…Françoise… .

How many people get to see a genius at work, eh?

I'm a very giving person.

(*Loudly.*) I'm a very giving person!

SABARTÉS: (*As himself.*) Hah!

PICASSO: What do you mean 'Hah!'? Hah?

SABARTÉS: (*Innocently.*) Were you 'giving' with Kahnweiler?

PICASSO: You'll be telling me next he was a philanthropist.

SABARTÉS: No. A businessman.

But a businessman who loves serious art. And serious artists.

PICASSO: (*Becoming his early self.*) A twenty per cent rise in the unit cost. Braque's work is fetching more than mine at auction. You're not doing your job.

SABARTÉS: (*As Kahnweiler.*) Braque paints fewer pictures. Therefore they are scarcer. Therefore they fetch more individually. Supply and demand.

PICASSO: Twenty per cent more. Supply and demand.

SABARTÉS: (*As Kahnveiler.*) You want to bankrupt me?

You paint fewer pictures like Braque: you get higher individual prices.

You paint more pictures. For which I create the clientele.

Therefore: you earn considerably more money than Braque.

You are free to choose. Three per cent.

PICASSO: You want to make me a pauper? Fifteen per cent.

SABARTÉS: (*As Kahnweiler.*) I'll think it over. We'll talk in the morning.

Three per cent you said?

(*As SABARTÉS.*) And so it would go.

PICASSO: I told you I liked him.

SABARTÉS: You liked the sound of your own voice, milking money.

PICASSO: I earned it. I had a reputation. I should be paid in accordance.

SABARTÉS: Hah!

PICASSO: What do you mean 'Hah!'? 'Hah'?

Is that any way to respond to the generosity of the genius who made you what your are today: immortal!

Who fed you, clothed you, kept you company from nineteen thirty-five until the day that you died!

Didn't I do your portrait, again and again?

Didn't I give you drawings, prints, paintings?

Didn't I allow you to meet the great and the good – through me!

Didn't I give you my most precious commodity: my time!

Didn't I give you your very reason for existence!

I rest my case.

SABARTÉS: (*Beat.*) Maybe so.

But what did you give the women?

PICASSO: (*Rattling them off.*) Sex. Money. Immortality. And Love.

SABARTÉS: (*Clicking his finger.*) 1938.

Lighting change.

The following 'telephone' sequence has a farcial edge. The geography of the different rooms can be suggested by four chairs in four different areas of the stage. PICASSO dashes from 'telephone' to 'telephone', the rhythm of the scene getting faster and faster until it comes to an abrupt hiatus with Françoise in 1960. Music can be used as a linking punctuation and should recall the 'military manoeuvres' of the Levée scene.

PICASSO: I'm going away.

SABARTÉS: Without lunch?

PICASSO: Away away. From here. You keep me posted on what's happening here.

(*Picks up phone.*) Paulo, I'm going to Juan-les-Pins for a holiday. See you soon, son.

SABARTÉS: (*To audience.*) Paulo is the son he occasionally bothers to see.

Olga is his mother, estranged from Pablo.

So Paulo will tell Olga, and Olga will holiday at Juan-les-Pins.

PICASSO: (*Phones.*) Marie-Thèrèse? I'll pick you up shortly, Okay?

SABARTÉS: Marie-Thèrèse is Picasso's mistress. Since she was sixteen.

She knows about Olga – Pablo's still married to her legally – which is why poor Pablo can't marry Marie-Thèrèse.

She doesn't know about –

PICASSO: (*Phoning.*) Dora, my sweet. I'm going away for a few days to work. Join me later. Marcel will pick you up. Byee!

SABARTÉS: (*To audience.*) Dora is his latest mistress. She knows about Olga.

She doesn't know about Marie-Thèrèse.

Pablo likes to amuse himself – in every sense…Marie-Thèrèse and he are on the beach…

PICASSO: (*SABARTÉS as Marie-Thèrèse, lies on the sand, all undulating curves.*) God, Marie-Thèrèse, you'd make a Spanish saint masturbate himself with desire. I can't keep my hands off you –

Olga! (*Feigning innocence.*) What are you doing here?

Olga! Don't kick Marie-Thèrèse! Olga!

You mustn't call Marie-Thèrèse a strumpet!

Marie-Thèrèse is not a whore!

Olga!

Leave this minute before I call the police!

(*To Marie-Thérèse.*) I'm so sorry my love. What terrible luck... Who'd have thought that she would be holidaying here at the same time as us!

Jumps up, then casually lights a cigarette and pours himself a glass of Evian water. Glances at his watch.

(*Seeing him.*) About time Marcel.

(*To audience.*) The chauffeur: you remember?

To SABARTÉS as Dora: an elegant bluestocking.

Dora, my sweet. How ravishing you look.

You'd make a Spanish saint masturbate himself with desire.

I can't keep my hands off you.

You like the hotel?

A quiet weekend with just the two of us. Let's go in for dinner.

Olga!

You can't say things like that to my friend Dora!

SABARTÉS: (*As himself: to audience.*) But she could. And she did!

1951.

PICASSO: (*Phones.*) Jacqueline. We're going off for the weekend.

SABARTÉS: (*To audience.*) Jacqueline is the latest mistress.

PICASSO: I'll be back sometime next week Françoise.

SABARTÉS: (*To audience.*) Françoise is the current mistress. He's living with her.

PICASSO: (*Phones.*) Marie-Thèrèse. I'll see you next Thursday as usual. Love you. Byee!

(*Phones.*) Geneviève? Fancy a day at Saint-Tropez?

You'd make a Spanish saint masturbate himself with desire!

I can't keep my hands from dreaming of you!

SABARTÉS: (*To audience.*) Remember the schoolgirl, Geneviève Laporte? She's back in the picture.

A very pretty young woman now.

PICASSO: (*Phones.*) Paulo. I'm going off to Saint Tropez for a long weekend. See you later, son.

SABARTÉS: Not counting the schoolgirls:

Uses the apartment at Rue La Boetie when he's in Paris…

Not counting the one-night stands with society women…

Not counting the casual come-ons when it takes his fancy. Not counting –

PICASSO rushes for the final phone, picks it up. He is knackered.

PICASSO: Aah!

SABARTÉS: (*To audience.*) 1960.

Drops phone onto hook.

Françoise had already done the unthinkable.

She had left Picasso!

Worse, she had married a Monsieur Luc Simon.

(*Phones as elderly lawyer.*) Could I speak to Madame Françoise, please?

PICASSO: (*As Françoise.*) Yes?

SABARTÉS: This is Maitre Bacque de Sariac, the lawyer for Monsieur Picasso. I am instructed to suggest the following to you.

Would you consider divorcing Monsieur Luc Simon?

That way, the status of your two children by Monsieur Picasso would be regularized.

You could then divorce, but the children would be legitimised.

PICASSO: (*As Françoise.*) …I…I need to think.

SABARTÉS: (*To audience.*) 1961. She agrees.

In January Claude and Palona are awarded their father's name.

In February –

PICASSO: (*As Françoise.*) Luc…I'd like a divorce…

SABARTÉS: March. Divorce proceedings have started. Françoise is sure that Picasso is going to remarry her. March the second. Picasso marries, in secret, *Jacqueline Roque.* Maitre de Sariac, who has not been informed, continues to clear the path for his client's marriage to Françoise.

Endgame.

PICASSO: She deserved it. Utterly selfish. Didn't I give her everything? And how did she repay me? She left me! Me! Picasso!

I couldn't work. She did that!

She poisoned the children against me.

She – stopped – Picasso – working.

No one does that! No one!

I did what had to be done.

I got my own back!

SABARTÉS: Really? And the other women?

PICASSO: For God's sake Sabartés, what are you rabbiting on about? So I slept with lots of women! What of it?

(*Points to audience.*) Do you think there's a single man here who wouldn't do what I did, if he had the opportunity? Eh?

(*To audience.*) You're all just jealous.

I didn't go looking for these women. They came to me. In droves.

So I availed myself. What man wouldn't?

It's only sex. I like sex. Lots of it. Regularly. It's my curse.

It's unreasonable to ask any one women to keep up with me, so naturally, I wouldn't want to burden any one of them. So I shared it out.

Where's the problem in that?

Look, it's not just men who like other partners.

Do you think Dora only slept with me?

She's had more men than a pig on a truffle-hunt.

(*Pointing to audience.*) Look at these women.

D'you think every woman here has only slept with one man apiece?

Wise up!

Fucking is good for you.

And with me it always stimulated work. Art. Serious work. Fucking good art.

So stop crowding me with all this moral bullshit.

It does not apply to me. Or to any serious artist, male or female. Sex is simply the engine oil for the motor. End of story.

Besides: you never upbraided me when you were alive, did you?

Never so much as mentioned morals!

(*Beat.*) You're not winning, are you Sabartés?

You never were much good at argument.

Not much good at anything, come to think of it, except at being my flunkey.

So be a good boy – and grow up!

A long beat: perhaps a percussive punctuation.

SABARTÉS: Exploiter. (*Calmly.*) I don't suppose you'd see yourself as malicious, spiteful, vindictive, venomous...

PICASSO: *I'm* not weak.

SABARTÉS: Exploiter: Isn't it a sign of weakness that you play with people, like a cat with a collection of mice.

PICASSO: In the real world there are mice and –

SABARTÉS: Exploiters?

PICASSO: Life eliminates the weak.

SABARTÉS: And death reverses the process.

PICASSO: Catholic superstition.

SABARTÉS: You're superstitious!

PICASSO: But I'm not religious.

SABARTÉS: You can't escape consequences.

PICASSO: What consequences? There aren't any.

I'm dead. You're dead. We're just the same as when we were alive.

Okay. So you get to play a few tricks.

You get to amuse yourself at my expense.

Real tough titty that, eh?

SABARTÉS: (*Coolly.*) 1945.

PICASSO: What of it?

SABARTÉS: Dora Maar. Beautiful –

PICASSO: Hypocrite. You hated her.

SABARTÉS: Beautiful. You were over sixty.

She must have thought that she was safe from predators.

Then along comes Françoise. Much younger. Beautiful.

Dora has a nervous collapse. Becomes suicidal.

But you knew all about that kind of thing, didn't you Pablo?

Olga had psychotic disturbances…because of you –

PICASSO: She was always unstable –

SABARTÉS: Then why did you marry her?

Everyone becomes unstable – if you drive them far enough –

PICASSO: I am not responsible for women going off their trolley –

SABARTÉS: Poor Dora: found sitting naked on the stairway to her apartment. Exploited.

PICASSO: Hard as nails; tough as an old boot.

You're not telling me she wasn't a strong woman.

SABARTÉS: But you broke her –

PICASSO: She broke herself.

SABARTÉS: She was being troublesome, wasn't she Pablo. So you sent her for electro-shock treatment.

PICASSO: And it cost me a packet, I can tell you.

I always paid. For everything.

Didn't I even give her a house in Ménerbes!

SABARTÉS: Be her.

PICASSO: (*Beat.*) No.

SABARTÉS: Depression. Be her.

PICASSO: (*Beat.*) No.

SABARTÉS: Be her.

PICASSO: N –

He is forced to become her: experiences the unseeing eyes and leaden weight of depression. Her body writhes as the electric current shoots through it.

SABARTÉS: (*Crouches down beside her.*)

(*Softly.*) Dora…Dora…I'm here to help you. I need to ask you some questions. Is that all right?

(*She nods.*) Jacques Lacan tells me you want to become a catholic. Is that correct?

PICASSO: (*As Dora.*) Yes.

SABARTÉS: You used to dislike religion…were a free spirit… You believed in enjoying sex, taking-

PICASSO: (*As Dora.*) That must have been somebody else…

SABARTÉS: They tell me that you paint still-lives now…quite traditional ones…

PICASSO: (*As Dora.*) Yes…it's restful…

SABARTÉS: Do you remember the kind of work you used to do?

The photographic experiments with Man Ray;

the First Surrealist Exhibition in London;

helping Picasso to work out the iconography of *Guernica* -

PICASSO: (*As Dora.*) Boring. I must have been a different person then…

SABARTÉS: (*Clicks his fingers.*) Well? Exploited?

PICASSO: You wee shite! I'm not res-[ponsible]

SABARTÉS: (*Clicks his fingers. PICASSO, anticipating, looks horrified.*) October 20, 1977. Night. Marie-Thèrèse's garage.

Marie-Thèrèse Walter is sixty-eight.

It is the fiftieth anniversary of her first meeting with Pablo Picasso. He picked her up, legally underage, innocent, outside a metro station.

She didn't even know whom he was…

Be her.

He is forced to become her. Picks up a length of rope. Throws it up.

Knots it. Stands on a chair. Puts around her own neck.

During the above the light narrows until it's just on her face.
SABARTÉS however is telling us Marie-Thérèse's thoughts.
Talking to herself.

'You were the only woman I ever loved'.

You wrote that Pablo. You were my Pablo. Always.

There was never anyone, anyone but you Pablo.

We had our 'little honeymoon' here, didn't we?

And soon, we'll have it again, my love.

Just you…and me…somewhere in this vast and echoing eternity… I'll find you Pablo…I'll search and I'll search until I find you, and then we'll be together again, for ever, my love.

She jumps, kicking chair over. Lights snap out. Snap on.
PICASSO/Marie-Thérèse is lying on the floor. He gets up,
rubbing his neck.

SABARTÉS: You're not responsible?

PICASSO: Of course not.

She loved me so much that she was prepared to die for me.

Touching.

I must have had *something*, for an exploiter, don't you think?

SABARTÉS: Picasso says, 'I must have had something'. What an epitaph! For an exploiter…

PICASSO: (*A beat as he realises that he has 'walked into it'.*) But on the other –

SABARTÉS: Jacqueline. October 15 –

PICASSO: No!

SABARTÉS: 1986.

PICASSO: No!

SABARTÉS: Three am.

PICASSO: N –

Forced to become her. She picks up a shotgun, walks calmly towards the chair, or the bed that Sabartés has wheeled out. She gets into the bed, pulls the sheet up to her neck. Her hand caresses the barrel of the shotgun.

At the start SABARTÉS utters the words, but soon PICASSO is pulled into becoming Jacqueline.

Sometimes I dream that you loved me Pablo…

I made myself love you…

Ironic, isn't it…to make a life…to devote a life, so absolutely to the whims of a man…

She lifts the shotgun, placing the barrel under her chin, her finger on the trigger.

I did everything –

PICASSO is now uttering the words. We hear SABARTÉS underneath but gradually he tails off until there is only the sound of PICASSO as Jacqueline.

– everything – that you asked…and more…

Your children I kept away from you, at your behest…

A long, long beat.

Every…abasement…of myself…I did…for you…

And I watched our children grow on the canvas, blossom in the frame, grow to maturity on the gallery walls, our children Pablo…my blood coursing in them…

But…it was…for nothing, wasn't it Pablo?

The world sees them as the offspring of a single, male parent…

All my love, devotion, as if for naught…

She grips the trigger tightly.

But I have always done my duty Pablo. Always.

To you and to our children. Duty.

She places the barrel of the gun in her mouth, sucks on it.

Light snaps out as the shot deafens us.

SABARTÉS: (*Beat.*) What's it like to blow your head off Pablo? To feel the steel rip apart the shards of your cranium, puncture the soft gristly tissues of the cortex, explode the synaptic charges of memory?

What's it like to be these women, and know…that there is no other way out?

Lost your tongue Pablo? How unusual…

PICASSO: Why-are-you-doing-this?

I thought that we were…friends…

SABARTÉS: (*Simply.*) We are.

I was….am…and always will be, your best – and only – true friend.

PICASSO: If that's being a friend, what the hell would you be like as my enemy?

Friend? Friend? You don't know the meaning of the word.

I was your friend.

(*Pacing.*) Don't tell me.

You wanted to give me a wider range of experiences.

All grist to the canvas, eh?

(*Becomes interested.*) Possible.

Canvas. Like a cubist head turned inside out.

(*Getting excited.*) Of course – Apollinaire in the trenches. Whee – shell, bang – splat!

Kostro trepanned. Memory exploding everywhere.

Palette knife slicing through a scumble of dirty greys.

Quarter inch paintbrush. Use the pointed tip of the handle and score, scrape and slash through the miasma. Squeeze a thick slobby splurge of pure cadmium red – slither through it with the fingers in an ejaculation of bloody memories!

It could work!

Yes!

It-could-work!

Beat.

Music: the tango.

Remember all those times…just you and me…no one else mattered…

Weren't you the one I talked to, showed the work to, discussed the work with…

Coming back home at midnight, after a round of the cafes…

Lighting change.

(*As his earlier self.*) I'll lock the doors!

Does so. Mimes hanging his hat on hatrack. PICASSO lifts off his hat, abruptly turns and tosses it to SABARTÉS who reflexively catches it.

SABARTÉS: (*Hangs his hat on the hat-rack. PICASSO does too.*) Now don't move!

Whips out small sketchbook and a pencil. Looking over his shoulder, then making one long continuous line on the sketchpad.

Sabartés as – Toreador!

Tears off paper.

(*Hands over paper to SABARTÉS.*) For you, old friend – a memento!

And now –

(*Starts to clean his teeth.*) Have a seat my dear sir. Pray tell me, your own inestimable opinion on the state of affairs of women's underwear!

Cut lighting change and music.

(*Beat. In the present.*) They were good days…weren't they?

SABARTÉS: I suppose they were…

PICASSO: You always believed in me. From the very start. No matter what.

And I always believed in you…in my own way…

SABARTÉS: Okay. Let's play.

PICASSO: (*Smelling a rat.*) Play? Really? Absolutely, indisputably, definitely – Yo!

We hear Debussy's music L'Après Midi d'un Faun.

A backdrop descends but close to the second wings. It is an abstracted version of a landscape in greys, russets and greens.

The Diagilev ballet. Hah! Bags I be Nijinsky, playing the Faun!

That means you're Olga, playing the nymph!

In time with the music SABARTÉS puts on a long pleated tunic of white muslin, stencilled with leaves, a long veil – and a wig of golden rope. The choreography is two-dimensional, like that of a Greek vase-painting. One arm across her breast, she crosses the stage in a rapid mechanical walk, then assumes a pose.

PICASSO puts on a small tail, adds a coil of vine leaves around his middle, then a cap of golden hair which has two horns on it. He finds a flute, picks it up, plays amusedly with its phallic possibilities, gives a tootle on it. Then he finds a bunch of grapes and assumes a pose. In sharp angular movements he squeezes a first, a second, then a third grape all over his face. He turns. The nymph, on seeing the Faun, raises her hands in surprise, fingers splayed, then scurries to the side. In sharp jumps and changes of direction, the Faun heads towards her, stops, drinks from a stream, then jumps across it, confronting her. Her hand goes to her mouth – startled – she half turns. His hand reaches out, grasping at her veil. She leaps off, leaving him with only the veil. He nuzzles it, lowers it, stretches it on the ground, then consummates his union with it, in a final taut jerk. The music suddenly stops.

SABARTÉS: You're not being true to your nature, are you?

PICASSO eyes him. Grins. Music starts again. The nymph, one arm across her breast, crosses the stage in a rapid mechanical movement. Then assumes a pose. In sharp angular movements, the Faun squeezes a grape all over his face, then pops another, slowly into his mouth. In sharp angular movements and changes of direction, he comes to the stream, feels the water, then leaps across, confronting her. Startled, she half-turns. He seizes her shoulder, turns her to face him, dominates her. He slowly pushes the grape out of his mouth, then into her mouth. He pulls the veil from her. Ties her hands with it. Thrusts her onto the floor and mounts her. Hard thrusting fury. Then he rolls off. Now he rises. Triumphant. One foot upon her recumbent body. Freeze-frame. Music stops.

He's full of himself.

Remember the Louvre?

The first living painter to be hung in that august establishment!

(*Grins.*) Of course, you gave ten paintings to the Musée d'Art Moderne!

PICASSO: Clever, wasn't I! So Georges Salles needed to humour me. '

Anything you want Monsieur Picasso?'

Well, I wouldn't mind seeing how my work stood up to the Masters.

So we went along. Me and Françoise…

(*As a favour.*) Will you be Françoise?

Lighting change. SABARTÉS nods. The following can be done with slide projections, if required. We should also be aware that the canvases are of different sizes: the Zurbaran is small, the Delacroix huge.

SABARTÉS: (*As Françoise.*) Where first Pablo?

PICASSO: Zurbaran. Put them near some Zurbarans, Monsieur Salles.

What do you think Françoise? Do they hold up?

SABARTÉS: (*As Françoise. Smiling.*) Yes.

PICASSO: They do, don't they?

(*Eagerly.*) Beside Delacroix.

(*To Françoise.*) That bastard. He's really good!

SABARTÉS: (*As Françoise.*) You survive Pablo. You survive. Triumphantly!

PICASSO: Velasquez. Put them beside Velasquez. Now there's a serious painter!

(*Delightedly.*) They're the same thing, aren't they! They're the same thing. The same thing. See! They're the very same thing!

Cut lighting change.

(*As himself now.*) I'm safe, amn't I? I really have survived. My work is…immortal?

SABARTÉS: Yes. Your work is immortal.

But at what cost?

PICASSO: Who cares about the cost?

I changed history, didn't I?

I changed the way people see!

I destroyed one point perspective.

I created masterworks like *Les Démoiselles D'Avignon, Guernica…*

He tails off as SABARTÉS stares intently at him.

SABARTÉS: *Les Démoiselles D'Avignon* –

PICASSO: You weren't there.

SABARTÉS: So?

PICASSO: We were just getting on so well…weren't we?

SABARTÉS: (*Flatly.*) Summer 1906. Gosol.

PICASSO: (*Surprised. And suspicious. Then brightly.*) Casanova rated it highly!

I painted *The Harem.*

SABARTÉS: You did indeed: four sumptuous nudes, all versions of Fernande; a paeon to sensual pleasure..and a response to Matisse's *Bonheur de Vivre* – you'd seen it a few months back at the *Salon des Indépéndents*.

Nothing quite like rising to a challenge.

Wouldn't want the old goat to get one over on you – would you?

PICASSO: So what's wrong with it?

SABARTÉS: Nothing. Absolutely nothing.

1907.

PICASSO: Oh…

SABARTÉS: Oh…

You were having problems with Fernande.

She couldn't have a child, could she? And you, with that insistent little pecker of yours, and that insistent little machismo, you wanted a little Pablo – a demonstration of your demanding virility.

PICASSO: Not so little.

SABARTÉS: What?

PICASSO: My pecker.

SABARTÉS: I was being ironic.

PICASSO: Oh…

Well I let her adopt a child, didn't I?

SABARTÉS: Indeed!

Now Fernande, she must be ever so stupid about art.

Why, in her memoirs, she never even mentioned *Les Démoiselles D'Avignon* once.

Therefore, she can't know much about art, can she?

PICASSO: I never said she didn't.

SABARTÉS: You were somewhat parsimonious, not to say misleading, about the information you *did* give to your biographers.

PICASSO: That's their problem, not mine.

My job is to produce works of art.

Their job is to research, and to write the truth!

SABARTÉS: Whose version of the truth?

PICASSO: Who cares? The more the merrier.

What's truth? I'll tell you what's truth.

Truth is whatever I want to believe at any particular moment.

Truth is *whoever* happens to be doing the looking.

Truth doesn't exist.

Satisfied? Biographer out of a job. Tough.

SABARTÉS: (*During the following, PICASSO is demonstrating: working on the floor.*) You were working on *Les Démoiselles D'Avignon.*

A flurry of preliminary sketches, suggesting five prostitutes, a sailor, and a bordello keeper.

Memories of Barcelona, Pablo?

Violence of colour. Violent simplification. Violent and brutal distortion.

What was going on in your head Pablo? Eh?

Oops! Dearie me! How could I be so blind!

This is another version of *The Harem,* isn't it Pablo?

But it's not a sweet, sensuous, warm, loving image, is it Pablo?

You're working on the canvas now, aren't you Pablo.

Venomously.

She's left you, hasn't she Pablo. She's walked out. Fernande has walked out. Why did she do that Pablo? She's a quiet, almost indolent, intelligent woman.

She's been living with you for years Pablo. You wanted her. You got her.

But she's walked out. Why Pablo?

Raymonde. That was her name, wasn't it?

The girl that the pair of you adopted.

What age was she? Fourteen? Thirteen?

PICASSO: (*Finds himself being forced to become his younger self.*) I'm not going to do – I'm not going to – I'm not –

Now he is locked into his younger self.

Raymonde. Yes...you pose very well; of course you do. Which of the portraits did you like best?

Ah! Different people model for me...

Of course you can help...there's no need to take your clothes...off.

(*Coming closer.*) You have the most beautiful breasts Raymonde. (*Takes out sketchbook.*) Just open your legs Raymonde...wider...

(*Sketching rapidly.*) I just need to... (*Leans forward, finger stretching out.*) help you to relax a bit more... (*Starts to take his trousers off with other hand.*) and then we could – (*Head turns sharply.*) Fernande!...

You're back early... Now don't be like that!

Come back! Now Fernande!

Standing up venomously, doing himself up, grabbing paintbrush and palette knife.

Stupid fucking woman. They're all the same –

Freezes in a violent attitude.

SABARTÉS: Heads based on African masks.

A woman squatting as if she's about to shit.

The men are removed.

This is Fernande, again and again, gutted,
cut up and re-assembled like a jigsaw,
hatred spewing across the canvas,
buttocks and breasts, orifices,
woman as the devil
an incantatory spell: primitive magic
strange beasts who need to be fucked –
once in a while – just to establish superiority –
of man.

Clicks his fingers: PICASSO unfreezes.

PICASSO: (*Seizing on a diversionary tactic.*) African masks?
I wasn't influenced by African masks. How could I be?
I knew nothing of African sculpture!

SABARTÉS: No? Strange…

I thought that Braque, Derain, Vlaminck and Matisse all
had African masks in their collections.

Of course, silly of me – you never met any of them, did
you?

And all those bric-a-brac dealers in the *Rue de Rennes*,
like *Pere Soulier* – perhaps you've never heard of the *Rue
de Rennes*, never even seen the *Rue de Rennes*, never even
strolled down the *Rue de Rennes* on a regular basis, and of

95

course you never bought work from *Père Soulier* did you, so you couldn't possibly have seen all those African heads in his shop, could you.

No, no, I stand corrected: the man with the most acute eye in Paris couldn't possibly have seen any African sculpture, could he?

(*Cheerfully.*) Shit always finds its own level, doesn't it!

PICASSO: So I can see!

SABARTÉS: I remember your mother saying:

'About you Pablo, I could believe anything. If some day, I was to be told that you had sung a high mass, then I'd believe that too!'

PICASSO: Leave my mother out of this.

SABARTÉS: Dutiful son, were we?

And then there's your dad.

Well?

PICASSO: He painted pigeons. Used to keep them.

SABARTÉS: You always kept pigeons.

PICASSO: And what does that prove?

SABARTÉS: Why don't you work it out? Consequences. For us both.

PICASSO: There aren't any Jaime.

SABARTÉS: Yes there are. 1961.

Remember?

Clutches his heart. Keels over. Lies as still as the dead.

A phone rings.

*PICASSO ignores it, looks up in irritated fashion, finally
answers.*

PICASSO: (*Irritably.*) Yes?

Who is it?

Mercedes? You haven't spoken to me in…

A stroke!

Which hospital. I'll be right round.

Approaches the sickbed.

You'll be fine Jaime. Of course you will. Won't you?

SABARTÉS: (*Having difficulty forming the words.*) Won't be
able to walk up eight flights of stairs to my apartment!

PICASSO: I'll buy you one with an elevator.

SABARTÉS: (*Getting up: to audience.*) And he did.

PICASSO: Bald head… Stooped like the rib of a beer
barrel. One arm paralysed.

One leg dragging after the other.

Every now and then you'd arrive at a *vernissage*: eyes
close up to my work, like suction pads!

And you kept on working: my honorary ambassador.

SABARTÉS: (*Still having difficulty in speaking – it's an effort.*)
Great news Pablo! At last. A Picasso Museum in
Barcelona!

And I'm to be the Honorary Curator!

Don't worry. When I'm dead, everything you've ever
given me will go there.

PICASSO: Dead? Dead? You'll never die Jaime. You're like
me. Immortal!

(*To audience.*) We talked on the phone almost daily. Wherever I was.

SABARTÉS: February the thirteenth, 1968.

Phone rings. PICASSO finally picks it up.

(*SABARTÉS as Doctor.*) Is that Monsieur Picasso? Good. This is Doctor Recamoin.

Monsieur Jaimes Sabartés has just succumbed to uraemic poisoning.

I'm afraid he's passed away.

PICASSO: (*To himself.*) He's not dead.

(*Flexes his wrist.*) I, Picasso, say: he is not dead. He *is*!

SABARTÉS: And he was. For Pablo.

From that day on, every print that he made, he dedicated to me as if I were still alive, and he sent it to the Picasso Museum in Barcelona.

If I stayed alive: so did he.

PICASSO: I *create*. I can make him live. I am Yahweh! I am God. I am creation.

I am and all shall be in a likeness to me. Me.

He *is*.

SABARTÉS: Time to go Pablo.

PICASSO: No! There's something I want to do.

Please Jaime…

SABARTÉS: What?

PICASSO: You've played me. Now I want to become you!

SABARTÉS: (*Beat.*) No.

PICASSO: You can't change the rules now Jaime. Come on. Please. Let me be you! You can be me.

SABARTÉS: If you insist.

PICASSO: I do!

(*To audience.*) Remember my verbal portrait of Jaime? When he died, it was in his wallet.

Now!

SABARTÉS: (*As PICASSO.*) Luminescent coal of friendship –

PICASSO: (*As SABARTÉS. To audience.*) I added my own lines...

An inextinguishable bonfire, flaming with the warmth of remembrance.

SABARTÉS: (*As PICASSO.*) Quickened by the breath of a kiss on the hand.

PICASSO: (*As SABARTÉS.*) Flame which no wind can possibly extinguish.

SABARTÉS: (*As PICASSO.*) As true in the telling as the certainty of a clock.

PICASSO: (*As SABARTÉS.*) Each dependent on the other.

A haven of peace, softness, tenderness, delight.

A throbbing heart...that delightful softness of the downy pillow inviting, oh so inviting...

Time for bed.

Pablo's in his room.

The glass striking marble: he's just finished gargling!

Toothbrush hitting the side of the glass...vibrating.

Taps turned off. Then the light.

Floorboards creaking as he pads to bed.

A cough. Then silence…

(*Suddenly breaking out as himself.*) Maybe I shouldn't go any further –

Becomes SABARTÉS again.

He shudders as if receiving unwelcoming news.

Finally his head sags.

Slowly he becomes PICASSO again.

You never told me Jaime. All those years.

All that…disapproval…yet you still…did *everything*…for me.

A flicker of hope from SABARTÉS.

PABLO takes out a sketchbook. Fiddles with it. Comes to a decision.

I've been idling up here. It's time I started work.

Let's do your portrait!

Like old times!

He lifts a pencil – but nothing happens. He tries to force it towards the page – but he can't. He tries again: nothing.

Jaime…Jaime…what's happening?

SABARTÉS: Consequences, Pablo, consequences.

For us both.

For you…this is your Hell.

Starts to walk away.

PICASSO: Where're you going Jaime? Come back!

We're going to talk aren't we? We've always talked.

Hardly a day when we haven't talked... Jaime...

SABARTÉS: (*He stops. His back to PABLO. Looks over his shoulder.*) I can't Pablo...no matter how much I want to. This is your Hell... (*Staring forlornly around him.*) and this, (*Exiting.*) is mine... (*Slowly exits.*)

PICASSO: (*Looking around him desperately as the lights begin to fade. A long ululating scream.*) No!

Now we can only see his face. He whimpers.

I have to work.

What am I, if I don't work?

Please...

(*Blackness. In the darkness, a last despairing.*) Please!

The eerie sound of wind, as if on a deserted street. A light illuminates the suspended heads of Fernande, Eva, Gaby, Olga, Marie-Thérèse, Dora, Françoise, Jacqueline – and SABARTÉS.

Blackout.

Art, Biography and Drama

Yo! Picasso! is the companion piece to the cycle of eight plays called *Picasso's Women*. Whereas the latter told the story from the point of view of each of the women in Picasso's life, the former tells the story from the point of view of Picasso and his biographer cum secretary Sabartés.

At this point, with reference to what the actors of both tended to refer to as a rather 'dense' and compressed text, I should touch on the relationship of art history and biography to drama. I myself operate at intervals as an art critic, art historian, and curator of art exhibitions. So I claim some knowledge of the thematics involved.

All of these plays, although using – and where possible adhering – to known facts, are not bound by them. While they are my attempts to recover the buried stories of the 'Picasso' women, and of Picasso himself, and thus provide alternatives to the tunnel visions of the Picasso Industry, they are, first and foremost, dramatic constructions. Their structure, their language and their emotional development, not to mention the whole apparatus of their characterisation, are specifically dramatic.

Audiences want to identify. Critical approaches keep one at a remove. Audiences wish to experience the complex emotional life of a character, be it the harrowing of tragedy or the riotous laughter of comedy. Critical approaches attempt to analyse, and dissect. The common ground of both is that they seek to understand their subject, but from very different angles of approach.

Put another way, these plays are *informed* by art criticism and biography. But as I happen to believe that most of what passes for biography or comment in the Picasso literature – especially with respect to the women in his life – is cursory in its attempts to understand them, one-sided in its attempts to evaluate them, and frequently downright speculative in its assumptions masquerading as facts, you'll have to forgive me if I have chosen to disagree radically with its conclusions.

It is important to remember that Picasso was, and still is, a multi-million pound industry. He was probably the first artist-millionaire, and he was certainly the first artist to achieve world-wide fame when he was still a relatively young man. It is not difficult to understand how critics, biographers and the like – mainly men – viewed the women – and the artist. Think of the groupies and hangers-on that surround today's pop stars, sports personalities and the like. Assumptions were made: that the women were only there to be 'seen'; that they were there for the money; that they were there to gain immortality by being portrayed by Picasso; that they were there for the sex.

Picasso was always a canny manipulator of people, and of the media. He played gallery against gallery, dealer against dealer, critic against critic, knowing just when to be magnanimous; and just when to cut off contact. To get access to him, to show his work, to be able to write about him at length (and often to be able, thus, to buy his work cheaply) was worth its weight in gold, and not just in terms of prestige.

Bearing this in mind, any given individual was unlikely to cause serious problems for the artist. Why kill the golden goose with unfavourable publicity? Women, after all, were just appendages to The Great Man. If there were conflicting views, whom would you believe? If any woman dared to voice a negative opinion, she was showered with abuse. Consider the reviews meted out to Françoise Gilot for her *Life With Picasso*; or, recently, to Arianna Stassinopoulos Huffington for her book on Picasso. Vilification would be putting it politely...

Of course most of the biographies are biographies of the *artist* which only incidentally discuss the women. Whereas a playwright, by nature of the job, trains himself to look at all sides of a personality, or a problem, often biographers only view individuals through the lens of their main character. Most books on Picasso take Picasso's side, assuming that everything Picasso says is true; and assuming that other accounts of incidents in Picasso's life, usually written about by males, are also true.

Even more remarkably, most Picasso biographers, memoirists and anecdote-scribblers fail to consider even the most rudimentary alternative interpretations. What is morally worse is the way in which they consistently downplay the grosser activities of their subject. Put another way, individual facts may or may not be correct in any given book on Picasso, but most of them are fiction when it comes to their 'analysis' of relationships and events.

I make no claims whatsoever as a biographer, as none of these plays aspires to biography. What I would, teasingly, suggest is that by trying to identify with the women in Picasso's life, these fictional plays present 'truer', more rounded portraits than those to be found in the tomes of Picasso 'scholarship'.

It is presumptuous of a man to try and enter the head of a woman, just as it is presumptuous of a woman to try and enter the head of a man. It is equally presumptuous for a playwright to enter the head of a great artist, or the heads of those associated with him. Playwrights however, indeed writers of all persuasions, have been exploring their presumptions for rather a long time. It is part of the job.

www.ingramcontent.com/pod-product-compliance
Ingram Content Group UK Ltd.
Pitfield, Milton Keynes, MK11 3LW, UK
UKHW020723280225
455688UK00012B/484